UNDER THE
SHADE OF
Grace

UNDER THE SHADE OF

Grace

Hearing God's Voice in the Secret Place

AMBER DESIREE DUNLEAVEY

Carpenter's Son Publishing

Cover and Interior Design by Suzanne Lawing

Edited by Robert Irvin

Printed in the United States of America

978-1-949572-44-5

Contents

Introduction

MY JOURNEY

The final curtain had fallen and the audience erupted in applause. I stood on the stage behind the curtain smiling, elated; the sound of the crowd pulsed through me. My friends and I had pulled off another amazing performance. We were certain: never in the history of theatrical production had Rogers and Hammerstein's *Oklahoma* been displayed so flawlessly! The dilapidated high school theater with creaking wooden floors and moth-eaten curtains was our Broadway, and we were its stars.

Now came the moment we waited for: the curtain call where we each received our greatest praise. One by one we took to center stage, bowing with dramatic flair as our grateful spectators whooped and applauded. As the last actor took his bow, we all held hands and bowed as one. At least sixty of us filled the stage, each one having at least one adoring fan in the crowd, most of us having many more. Parents, grandparents, sisters and brothers, teachers, peers, and secret crushes all lifted their voices, shouting "Attaboy!" to their loved ones on stage. The roar was deafening, and the lights were so blinding we could hardly make out the silhouettes of the individuals in the first row, let alone find the faces of those we cherished in the audience.

And yet, I heard it. In the midst of that roaring crowd, I heard my father's voice call my name. And my heart smiled.

When we are familiar with a voice, it's easy to recognize it, even in the midst of tumult. We can recognize the emotion, the passion, the questions in a voice, simply because we are intimately acquainted with the one who speaks. If my father said my name in a serious, longer tone, I knew I had better watch myself. If he said my name with a brightness, like during this moment onstage, I knew he was proud of me and saying my name in approval. The same word was spoken, but with entirely different meanings. This is the power of knowing my father's voice.

If there is power in knowing my earthly father's voice, how much more so my heavenly Father? John's gospel tells us over and over again that Jesus is the voice of our heavenly Father, the very Word of God (John 1:1, 5:19-30, 7:16-18, 12:49, 17:8). John 10:4 says that when Jesus speaks, His followers know His voice. *The Message* version says it like this: "He (Jesus) leads them and they follow because they are *familiar* with his voice" (emphasis mine). Part of the blessing of being a child of God is we are each given the ability to become familiar with His voice. We all heard the Father call us at salvation, so we've been given ears to hear Him. Through an ongoing relationship, we learn more about His heart, His nature, His likes and dislikes—and we become mature to the place where we can recognize His voice above all others, even in the midst of a roaring crowd. But every good Christian also knows we all have just flat-out missed hearing Him. We've thought we heard God, we've thought we obeyed God, only to find ourselves in a situation where we are

I KNOW HOW I STARTED OUT BELIEVING I HEARD FROM GOD, ONLY TO FIND MYSELF SAYING, "OOPS." IF ANYONE CAN SHAKE MY CONFIDENCE IN MYSELF, IT'S ME.

left scratching our head, saying, "How in the world did I end up here?"

Many believers lack confidence in their ability to hear God. I know I have. The problem with me is this: I know myself. I know my faults. I know my failures. I know how I started out believing I heard from God, only to find myself saying, "Oops." If anyone can shake my confidence in myself, it's me.

That's why it's ironic that on many occasions I am certain I have heard His voice. Was it by faith? Absolutely. Was it still followed by doubts? You bet. But somehow, in that moment, I still believed I heard Him. Little ole imperfect me heard great big, perfect God. Even more ironic is that one time, while seeking the Lord for direction, I believe I heard Him say to me, "What if you dared to believe that you, as my child, really do hear my voice?" Do you know what God was implying here? He wasn't just correcting my unbelief. He wasn't just encouraging me. He was reminding me of my identity: *I'm His kid.*

I believe the enemy puts more doubt on the believer's ability to hear God than almost any other area of faith because the more we hear the Father's voice, the more our identity as sons and daughters of God is awakened. Also, the more of God we hear, the more God's identity is revealed to us as well. It's a double blessing! We learn more about who we are in Christ as we learn about who Christ is in us. It's an eternal cycle of discovering!

THE TREES IN THE GARDEN

God has always been a communicator, someone who loves to dialogue and interact with His family. We find this truth at the very beginning of creation. Genesis 1:26 records the conversation of God with His Son as He excitedly announces the making of their crowning creation, mankind. I can imagine the Father's beautiful eyes gleaming with pleasure as He turns to His Son and says, "It's time. Let's do it! Let us make man in our image!" Oh, the rejoicing that must have erupted that sacred day! The Bible says God Himself planted a garden for man to enjoy, complete with a very special tree for them to eat from called the Tree of Life (Genesis 2:8, 9). The Scripture makes it clear that this tree was given to mankind to enjoy and eat from daily (Genesis 2:9, 3:22). Once man was made, we find that God would meet with Adam and Eve in the garden "in the cool of the day," quite possibly under the shade of this Tree of Life (Genesis 3:8). I imagine God casually strolling with them under its large outstretched branches, teaching them about nature, science, colors, and music. It was a natural conversation between God and His created family. Something He loved to do every day in the garden of Eden.

"IT'S TIME. LET'S DO IT! LET US MAKE MAN IN OUR IMAGE!" OH, THE REJOICING THAT MUST HAVE ERUPTED THAT SACRED DAY!

But it was in this garden that we also find another mysterious tree: the Tree of the Knowledge of Good and Evil. It was the one tree from whose fruit God instructed man to *not* eat. I will not try to expound a deep theological explanation for why this tree was planted except to say that I believe obedience and love without a choice *to* obey or *to* love isn't obedience or love at all. God gave man the beautiful gift of choice, of free will—to choose to love Him, or to choose not to, through disobedience. The existence of this tree is a mystery for which I do not have all the answers. This much I am certain of, however: it was under the shade of *this* tree that we find Satan first casting two shadows of doubt that still hover over God's children.

Genesis 3 tells us that Satan posed a question to Eve, a question of doubt and uncertainty: "Did God really say . . . ?" (Genesis 3:1) This first shadow of doubt was one that questioned our ability to know if we had heard God correctly. Then, when Eve had been hooked by doubt, He cast the next shadow. I can imagine him leaning on the trunk of the Tree of the Knowledge of Good and Evil as he explains—deceptively—to Eve how she can "become like God" (Genesis 3:5).

Notice, among all creation in the garden that day, only two individuals were *already* like God—the ones God made in His likeness, Adam and Eve. And yet, this very fact was what Satan convinced them both to question: their identity as God's children.

So here we find, in the very inauguration of recorded time, the same shadows of doubt that still plague many of our minds today: Did God really speak to me? Am I really qualified to hear Him? Do I really belong to Him, and does He really belong to me? It's as if all of mankind is held in blackest shadows under the branches of the Tree of Knowledge as these questions weigh down our souls. These are questions that have plagued us since time's beginning.

However, it's in another beginning of sorts that we find the brightest light chasing these shadows of doubt away. It's the beginning of Jesus' ministry, and Matthew 3:13-17 says that Jesus goes to the Jordan River to be baptized. Jesus enters the muddy waters, and His cousin John plunges Him beneath the stream. As He comes up out of the river, the voice of the Father pierces the sky: "This is My beloved Son in whom I am well pleased" (John 3:17, NKJV). Now, up to this point, not much has been recorded about Jesus' adult life. Matthew tells of His birth in the first two chapters of his book, and Matthew then begins chapter 3 with Jesus' ministerial inauguration day at the Jordan. There have been no miracles, no healings, no feedings of the multitude, and definitely no cross. For all accounts and purposes, there is not one "special" thing Jesus has done (outside of plain obedience) to make us think this Heaven-opening, dove-descending, angels-singing should occur. And yet God chose *this* moment to speak audibly to His Son these needed words of affirmation.

There are probably countless reasons God chose this moment. This much I know: God was making it abundantly clear that He isn't pleased with us simply because of what we do, for Jesus was just beginning His ministry. He was telling Jesus, "You are my Son. That is enough for you to be. That is enough for me to love you." Before He had raised the dead or been raised Himself, Jesus had the pleasure of God over

His life simply because He was a child of God. Oh, how this must have carried His heart as He entered the desert for forty days of great temptation. How it must have sustained Him those three incredibly arduous years of ministry knowing that He didn't have to work to *gain* His Father's approval. No, He worked from a place of approval. It's a totally different mind-set.

This same sustaining grace is given to us today. God wants us to be confident in hearing Him speak and confident in our position in His family. As we hear our Father speak, something inside of us comes alive: Our hope! Our calling! Our confidence grows as the Spirit of adoption calls our name and we once again eat of the fruit of the Tree of Life. This is why Satan does everything He can to call us away from the shade of grace and keep us in doubt under the blackening shade of the Tree of Knowledge: to cripple our identity in Christ.

LISTENING LESSONS

This is also why, I believe, God speaks in many different ways. He deeply desires us to know who we are in Him, so He speaks in a variety of ways: through nature, through His Word, through godly counsel, through impressions and feelings. Another way He speaks is through visions and dreams. I remember first taking note of my dreams as a child. My first dream that I knew was different was one in which I was sharing the gospel with my neighbor when, all at once, music surrounded us, and I was caught up in the air, hovering with the sounds of Heaven all around me. I knew it was a special dream, but at the time I had no grid for interpreting.

A few years later I saw Christ in a dream for the first time. I dreamed that my youth group and I were praying for revival in a large room that had doors all around the walls. A fellow student entered the room and excitedly said, "I've just seen Jesus!" We were all so thrilled and believed our prayers were working. After rejoicing, we settled back into a mode of prayer. I, however, was drawn to a door in front of me.

With the sounds of my peers' prayers filling my ears, I reached out and opened the door. Suddenly, a bright light shone down and I could make out, though barely, the image of Jesus hanging on the cross. The light was shining from His face so brightly that I could really only see Him from the legs down. I dropped to my knees and, as the light from His face touched the other students, they too bowed in worship. Then the dream ended.

This time the dream so radically shook me that I told my parents and youth leader about it. I decided to tell my parents first. I was a bit nervous to share this experience with them, but the dream was so profound, I felt I had to let them know. So, I waited until what I thought, in my pre-teen estimation, was the best moment to tell them: at The Hickory Pit, our small town's local BBQ joint. I sat working up my nerve to tell them while they enjoyed their pulled-pork sandwiches and then finally, with a deep breath filling my lungs, I bravely shared the dream in all its detail and then paused to bite my lip in nervous anticipation of what they would say in response. But my parents didn't really know what to make of it. Although I had a Spirit-filled upbringing, these kinds of experiences weren't openly encouraged, let alone discussed, in our house. As I told them, I expected . . . well, I expected . . . something. I don't know what exactly. Instead, it was more like, "Oh, wow, that's nice! Pass the barbecue sauce." I remember feeling perplexed and unsure of myself in that moment. But when I told my youth leader, He had me share it with my small youth group. I remember timidly sharing my dream with them, but I believed the passion of what I saw would begin to burn in them as I spoke. I just knew God was calling us to pray for revival and that every one of us would see His face if we did! As I watched their faces, it was clear, however, that they had the same reaction as my parents.

It would have been extremely easy, after my initial experience with others, to dismiss my dreams as nothing more than indigestion. I don't blame my parents or my youth group for any wrongdoing. They responded just as I have on many occasions when someone presents

ONE THING I DO KNOW: GOD HAS A SENSE OF HUMOR IN GETTING ME TO GROW IN CONFIDENCE.

me with something I cannot explain or something I just don't know what to do with. I am so grateful, however, that something inside of me could not shake those dreams. To this day I can remember the dreams God gave me throughout my life. This does not, however, mean that I always know what He is saying through them. And, unfortunately, it also doesn't mean I am fully confident in hearing when I do receive them.

One thing I do know: God has a sense of humor in getting me to grow in confidence. As I began to step out in more belief that I had heard His voice, I had a dream that highlighted my insecurities. I dreamed I was invited to a roundtable discussion among prophets. I gladly accepted the honor but had no expectations. As all the prophetic people gathered around the table, a well-known prophet sat across from me. He looked at me in surprise and said, "What is she doing here? She can hardly hear." Everyone around the table gasped in shock at the prophet's harsh words. Everyone, that is, but me. I sat there nodding my head in agreement with him. "Yep. He's right," I was saying. "I can hardly hear at all."

I woke up quite surprised. God really had my attention on this one. This particular prophet offered a dream interpretation school. I emailed the school my dream, but I expected them to say, "Looks like you should stop trying altogether." However, I was shocked to hear their reply, and not from one interpreter, but from two, and on two separate occasions. The interpreters explained that God wasn't telling me that I was inadequate in hearing; He was showing me that *I* believed I couldn't hear. I was invited to that table because I *could* hear, not because I couldn't. I had produced the fruit of hearing and was therefore invited to participate with the others. I was so intimidated, however, by the big shot, super-hearer prophet before me that

I compared my gift to his, which the Bible tells us is foolishness. I felt I could never measure up to him. I believed the negative voice of the prophet over the voice of the Spirit in my life. I was agreeing with a lie.

God was using His light of revelation to chase away the shadows of doubt cast from Eden's fall. Some time after this dream, while my husband and I were driving to the mall one day, I was in the passenger seat praying inwardly to God for encounters with Him. I was saying, "God, I want to hear you! I want you to speak to me! I want open visons! I want angelic encounters!" God impressed, and loudly, on my heart, "Desiree, you have angelic encounters! You've seen them in your dreams!" I replied, "But, God, they are only in my dreams!" Patiently, the voice of the Lord replied, "And so were the angels in Joseph's dreams." I suddenly remembered that many heroes in the Bible had powerful encounters through their dreams. How easy it could have been for Joseph or Daniel to dismiss their dreams. But God shaped history through them because they simply believed.

> I WRESTLED WITH THE IDEA OF REALLY, *REALLY* BELIEVING THE THINGS I WAS SEEING IN MY DREAMS, NOT TO MENTION THE THINGS I WAS SEEING IN MY MIND'S EYE WHILE PRAYING AND WORSHIPING.

But could I really believe that God was shaping my personal history in the same way? Who was I, after all, that He would speak to me like my biblical heroes? I wrestled with the idea of really, *really* believing the things I was seeing in my dreams, not to mention the things I was seeing in my mind's eye while praying and worshiping. The longer I walked with the Lord, hungering for who He is, the more I found myself watching scenes unfold in my heart while in His presence. I wrestled with this because I didn't have too many people in my life who seemed to have similar experiences. Sure, the people in the Bible had visions, but they were untouchable to me—incomparable to who I was as a little nobody. However, the things I was seeing were so powerful I couldn't deny that *something* was happening.

One particular time I was asking the Lord to help me sense Him throughout my day, a reoccurring prayer in my life. As I sat with eyes closed, an image of a large Jewish papa appeared in my mind. Like Tevye from *Fiddler on the Roof,* this papa had broad shoulders and a long graying beard. He was seated on a weathered wooden bench that accompanied an aging timber table that was situated in a similarly simple room. Few decorations adorned the walls. Fewer fine furnishings graced the room. Yet there was a beauty in this room that no words could adequately describe. It was a warmth of emotion, something that communicates to the soul that radiated from this father, filling the room. A perfectly contented smile rested on the father's face. The source of his contentment was found in the goal of his gaze. His eyes were fixed on a child playing with wooden blocks on the floor before him, a child perfectly satisfied in his play, surrounded by a home overflowing with love and acceptance. As I gazed on this image in my mind's eye, I heard the Lord say, "This is the feeling I want you to remember when you want to know how to connect with my heart during your day." I knew in that moment that this image was revealing God as my Jewish Papa simply taking delight in me taking delight in Him. Who could deny this picture or the other things I saw in prayer? Who could deny this emotion I was sensing or the things I was hearing? These images were as real to me as anything I had ever experienced.

PERMISSION TO BELIEVE

After the image of God sitting at a table fully pleased with me, or the dream of being invited to a prophetic roundtable, I wish I could say I simply started believing, that I lived free from all doubts. Alas, I did not. Years later, I was sitting at a real table with a highly prophetic hero of mine. I had been hanging on his crazy stories with bated breath. His stories were so amazing: seeing Jesus with his naked eyes, open visions, angelic visitations! This guy was the kind of hearer and seer I dreamed of becoming! Not only that, He had a quiet, unshakeable confidence in his sonship. He talked and shared in such a way that displayed his absolute love for the Father and absolute love for being His child. Occasionally, I would tell him a story of my own. I was confident enough by this point in my life to share my encounters, dreams, my own still-small voice impressions with him. In truth, however, I downplayed each one by introducing it with the phrase, "I know it's subjective, but I believe God said . . . " Finally, after the third time of couching my experiences with that phrase, my hero said, "Why are you doing that? What does that even mean? Just believe you're hearing and that your experiences are real!"

"WHY ARE YOU DOING THAT? WHAT DOES THAT EVEN MEAN? JUST BELIEVE YOU'RE HEARING AND THAT YOUR EXPERIENCES ARE REAL!"

I was floored. Shocked. Could this great man really be giving me permission to believe I could hear? My earlier dream of the prophet sitting across from me saying I could not hear was now replaced with the reality of this prophet saying, "Simply believe." What's sad, however, is that God had been saying this to me for years: "You're my daughter in whom I am well pleased. Now . . . simply believe."

This permission to believe went to a deeper level when I began to seriously journal my prayers with God. I had been journaling with Him for years, but when I discovered Mark Virkler's book, *How to Hear God's Voice*, I felt both validated in what I had been doing and also better equipped to launch out in that medium like never before. Enough praise truly cannot be given for Virkler's book. So much growth has sprung forth in my life because of Virkler's teachings. When I found his book, I had just finished reading a wonderful book called *You May*

All Prophesy by Steve Thompson. This book stirred up a hunger in me to know more about how to hear God's voice and how to teach others to do the same. I decided to teach a Sunday school class on the topic of hearing God, but I also knew I needed to do a little more personal study. Through a search on the Internet, I came across *How to Hear God's Voice*. I didn't know anything about Mark Virkler, so I decided to do a bit of research on him too. In my searching, I found that men that I honored as true believers, men such as John Arnott and Jim Goll, had associated themselves with Virkler. This gave me a peace to know there was most likely a strong legitimacy to his ministry! Now I had no concerns about purchasing the book and quickly did just that.

As I read and studied Virkler's book, I was introduced to his profoundly simple approach to hearing God speak. This approach is based on Habakkuk 2:1, 2, which reads: "I will stand on my guard post and station myself on the rampart; And I will keep watch to see what He will speak to me . . . Then the Lord answered me and said, 'Record the vision . . . '"(NASB). Virkler teaches that in order to hear God, a believer must quiet themselves in His presence (stand on their guard post), fix the eyes of their heart on Jesus (watch to see what He will speak), expect to literally see what He shows that believer, understand that His voice often sounds like spontaneous thoughts, and then write down what is seen and heard (record the vision). This obviously takes us to a point of stepping out in faith and believing that what we are seeing and hearing will be directed by the Holy Spirit.[1]

Being a student of the Word, I knew that God used visions over and over to speak to His children, and I was accustomed to seeing pictures painted on my mind's eye during prayer or worship. And since I was already journaling some of my prayers and visions, it only made sense to combine the two experiences. Still, this was the first time I had ever thought about taking my journal in hand, closing my eyes, and expecting God to, well . . . simply talk to me! It was an exciting idea, but also an unnerving one. Anxious questions filled my mind: What if I made a mistake? What if I assumed things were from God when they were just from me? Or worse: what if they're from Satan? Would I be able to know God's voice from my own or the enemy's?

Thankfully, *How to Hear God's Voice* doesn't simply teach believers how to step out in greater levels of hearing, it also teaches precautions and guidelines to use when journaling in this manner. For instance, when approaching God in this way, we must always come with a pure heart, confess any sin that He reveals to us, and any areas of disobedience, unforgiveness, or other weights that would hinder us from rightly approaching God or hearing His voice. We always approach God based on the blood of His Son, Jesus. Beginning at the cross during our prayer time, then, is a great refuge from the voice of Satan or the voice of self. Also, journaling will always align with God's Word, never going against Scripture and certainly never replacing it or being equal to it. Journaling is subjective because it is never totally free from self; therefore, we are to test the Word, as Scripture tells us, by sharing it with two or three mature believers (1 Corinthians 14:29).

I took Virkler's words to heart. As I read through the book, I journaled along at the end of the chapters, stepping out in ways I had not pursued before. I submitted myself to a few spiritual advisors—my husband, also my pastor's wife, and another, a godly lay minister. Each week I submitted to them what I was hearing from God. They were all willing to give me their time and their prayers, which was awesome. To this day, I submit my journals and visions to other believers. Having advisors in my life gives me an assurance of hearing God that I cannot have on my own.

WHEN I WANT TO CONNECT WITH THE SPIRIT INSIDE ME, I MUST BECOME STILL IN ORDER TO DO SO.

Truly, the Lord wants us connected to His body for our own good. It gives a peace of mind and a sense of unity to be able to share with others what God is speaking. Through submitting my journals to others, I have found an increased desire in my life to be connected with other people in the body of Christ. They are also a huge encouragement to my life. One spiritual advisor told me she strongly felt that God had been waiting for me to discover this technique of dialoguing with him! I even had a dream that Cindy Jacobs, someone I highly respect in hearing God's voice, came to me and told me I needed to read and keep reading Virkler's book. What an encouragement!

When I want to connect with the Spirit inside me, I must become still in order to do so. I have found there are a few ways to become still in my life: I listen to music, I fix my eyes on Jesus, I pray in tongues, or I sing a song. Sometimes, I do them all at once to quiet myself, while at other times I find I only need to use one technique. I love to pray in nature. Going for a walk or just staring at the stars has always connected me to the throne room inside my heart. I can sense God's presence every time I take the time to notice His beautiful creation. Just learning how to abide has really aided me in coming to stillness. I have found since I began journaling with God that it is easier to abide in His presence and come to stillness. Some days, it's like I wake up with an awareness of God all around. These days are becoming more and more natural! I am always amazed when all I have to do to tune to the Spirit in me is take a deep breath and close my eyes. He is so faithful to remain and rest inside of us!

THERE ARE SO MANY FACETS TO THE LORD. HE IS FATHER, HE IS BROTHER, HE IS HUSBAND, HE IS FRIEND.

To equip you to begin a journey of journaling your conversations with God, I encourage you to read Steve Thompson's book *You May All Prophesy* and Mark Virkler's *How to Hear God's Voice*. From my very first prayer journal entry, I was so surprised at how tenderly God spoke to me. I was shocked at how loving and how fun He often was! There are still times when He just makes me laugh at the things He shows me! He is just like a dad: making me laugh, picking me up, playing around. Think of it: if He's the King of

Kings and Lord of Lords, well, then, He must be the Dad of Dads! And oh, how He has revealed this to me. He loves His children deeply. He corrects us compassionately. He trains us righteously. He is such a good Father. To me, He most often reveals Himself in a gentle way, as the One who says, "Come to me, all you who labor and are heavy laden, and I will give you rest" (Matthew 11:28). And almost every time I sit down to journal with Him, I weep for adoration as I catch another glimpse of His heart.

There are so many facets to the Lord. He is Father, He is Brother, He is Husband, He is Friend. He is the holy, the righteous, the blameless One. He is humble and lowly, yet He is high and lifted up. He dwells in unapproachable light and yet He is fully approachable. Let me say it again: He is a *fully approachable* God.

WHAT DISOBEDIENCE COST IN EDEN, OBEDIENCE REQUIRED IN GETHSEMANE.

This is the lesson God tried to teach us in the Garden of Eden. But when we failed to grasp it, He came and taught us again in another garden: the Garden of Gethsemane. Here we find the Christ, the Son of the Living God, wrestling with the shadows of doubt that Satan cast over creation, crying out to the Father in His hour of great trial (Matthew 26:36-42; Luke 22:44; John 18:1-11). Here we see Him choose to obey the Father at the cost of His own life. What disobedience cost in Eden, obedience required in Gethsemane.

From the first garden, man was sorrowfully excommunicated by God (Genesis 3:22-24). In the second garden, God was angrily excommunicated by man (John 18:1-13). One was led away from a tree while the Other was led to a tree. I'm sure on that day Satan was once again leaning on the trunk of the Tree of the Knowledge of Good and Evil maniacally laughing in what he thought was his eternal victory. After all, this tree had cast its shadows over all of history until that very moment. Never could Satan have imagined that it would be another tree that would uproot his victory. For as Christ was lifted up on the tree on a hill called Calvary, He took upon Himself every sin, every iniquity, and every effect that the Knowledge of Good and Evil had caused since the fall in the garden (Galatians 3:13). It was on *this tree*—Calvary's tree—that Christ washed away the sin and shame of Eden's fall and, when He rose again three days later, He rose as the Tree of Life for everyone who will believe in Him! When He rose, He cast His eternal light over a darkened world, freeing those who would follow Him from the shadows of doubt forever (John 1:4, 5, 9-13; 12:46; 15:5). Now it is His branches—His outstretched arms of love—and the shade of His cross that I run to and find my rest (Psalm 91:1, 4; Song of Solomon 2:3). It is here that I commune with Him just as Adam first did in Eden: face to face and friend to friend.

Normally when I sit down and close my eyes to journal, I see Him with the eyes of my heart, resting under a beautiful tree. Here, underneath this tree, Jesus teaches me to hear His voice; He teaches me about who He is and who I am in His eyes. From this tree have come the greatest lessons of my life. Here, under the canopy of His tree, He shines His light of revelation and love and dispels the shadows of doubt and fear. In the garden of my heart, He silences the serpent's questions and empowers me to simply believe.

PLEASE NOTE THAT ALTHOUGH THIS BOOK RECORDS MY CONVERSATIONS WITH THE LORD IN CASUAL STYLE, I AM IN NO WAY DECLARING, WORD FOR WORD, "THUS SAITH THE LORD."

Come with me and sit a spell under the shade of this marvelous, glorious tree. Here the Father will teach us to know His voice and trust His ways. Each chapter before you is an invitation into the garden of prayer, where lessons on how to launch out into greater belief await you. Each chapter is designed to shed light on the two shadows of doubt that Satan brings against us: the doubt of what God said and the doubt of who we are in Him. At the end of each chapter are key points for recognizing when and how God speaks as well as the personal ways that God awakens confidence in us in our position as sons and daughters.

I pray as my personal journey of growing in confidence unfolds in these pages you will find your own heart encouraged by what God revealed to me. Please note that although this book records my conversations with the Lord in casual style, I am in no way declaring, word for word, "Thus saith the Lord." Every word is to be tested and weighed in the light of the Bible and by the witness of the Holy Spirit inside of us. These words are not Scripture and these words are not fully accurate for we all "know *in part* and prophesy *in part*" (1 Corinthians 13:9).

On the other hand, I encourage you to launch out into your "part"! There *is* a part of prophesy for us "all," and there is knowledge we can all learn directly from the Holy Spirit in partnership with His written Word. I encourage every reader to launch out into the casual conversation that the Lord desires each of us to enjoy with Him! He wants us all to become familiar with His voice, for when we do we will find ourselves becoming more and more alive to who He is and who He has made us to be. As we come to this place of maturing confidence, whether on the brightest morning or the darkest night of our life, we will find ourselves standing center stage and hear the applause of Heaven roaring around us. Our hearts will bow before Him and we will come alive as we listen through the crowd and hear that sweet, familiar voice calling our names. The voice of our Father, saying: "You are my beloved child. Well done."

Come with me now and rest in His love as together we learn life-giving lessons under the Shade of Grace.

GETTING STARTED

If you are new to prayer, to journaling, or to stepping out in faith to hear God, there are some basic things you can do to get started.

1. **Commit your heart to Jesus.** If you have not started a relationship with God the Father through Jesus, now is a great time to start. The Bible says that every single person on the planet has sinned (Romans 3:23). But it also says that if we confess our sins, God is faithful to forgive us our sins because of the death and resurrection of Jesus. If you believe that Jesus died for your sins, that He is the Son of God who God raised from the dead, then you will be changed from the inside out! Pray a simple prayer asking him to remove your sins and be Lord of your life. You can pray something as simple as this: "Jesus, I know I am a sinner. I know you died to make me clean and right with God. Come be my Lord and my very best friend."

2. Whether you just committed yourself to Jesus or whether you have followed Him for fifty years, **believe Jesus' promise is for you**: His sheep know His voice! Simply take God at His Word and believe that you have been brought into fellowship with God through faith in Christ—a fellowship that includes conversing and communing with your Father.

3. **Get alone with God, away from distractions that would pull your focus away.** While praying throughout your day is an awesome way to connect with God, a focused, set time of quiet prayer is vital in learning how to discern God's voice. If you set the same time and place each day, you will find that prayer comes more readily and naturally over time. Remember: it's all about spending time together! If you miss your prayer time, it's OK. Just pick up the conversation again! But do know that a scheduled prayer time will help you keep that conversation going.

4. If your mind starts racing with things you need to do (i.e., taking out the trash, making that call), **try writing a to-do list, and**

then set it aside. This way, your mind can rest in knowing that you will remember your tasks. If you do get distracted, do not fall into condemnation. Just pick up where you left off! God is a good friend who knows that "life happens." He is always ready to pick up the conversation again.

5. **If your mind starts racing with sins you have committed, make sure you have repented of them.** Go to the cross and ask God if you have failed to repent of this sin. If so, ask God to cleanse you! If you have already repented of them, then think about the cross of Christ and praise God that you are forgiven. Remember, God will not remind you of something He has already forgotten—and He has forgotten your sin! Thoughts of past sins that are already forgiven are not from God—they are from the enemy. Take them captive by praising God and thinking on His goodness, using Scripture to restore your confidence.

6. **Remember that conversation is a two-way street!** When you pray, don't do all the talking. Quiet yourself and pause to listen to what the Spirit might be saying. Take a journal and a pen with you (or even sit at your computer) and, by faith, write down what you feel you hear or see. Remember, it's by faith! Give it a try!

7. **Close your eyes when you pray.** Imagine a serene picture like an oceanside or a rolling hill. Ask the Holy Spirit to give you impressions and pictures. Even if it is small, even if it is a flash, write it down and ask God to expound on it. Close your eyes at times while you are reading your Bible. Imagine the scene you are reading about and ask the Holy Spirit to show you truth in visual form.

Chapter 1

LESSONS FROM THE GARDEN

As long as I can remember, I've had a deep love for nature in all its forms: rolling hills, buzzing bees, fragrant flowers, and even gathering storms have always captured my attention. This love for nature is deep because the roots of this affection began in my infancy. Some of my earliest memories come from my three-year-old experiences of running in the lush green grass that blanketed my grandparents' backyard. It was cool and thick under my chubby bare feet, as thick as any carpet I have ever seen. The luscious lawn was canopied by towering sycamore trees whose gray bark peeled like ribbons and whose branches overshadowed the landscape, offering a respite from the summer sun or a magical, sparkling canopy in the winter snow.

It was a fascinating world to me, a world that seemed to roll on endlessly, although I am certain the property line stopped just past the mossy pond that abutted the estate. And while my grandparents' yard held my imagination captive, my own backyard also brought another kind of enchantment. Outside my back door was a deeply wooded area filled with babbling streams, quiet ponds, timid deer, and gigantic oaks—an interminable canvas for my young imagination. Closing the door on the ordinary, I would venture outside where the extraordinary awaited me. Pausing on my aging deck, drinking in the sights of the woods beyond my backyard, I breathed deeply as I stood at the doorway of imagination, a smile resting on my face. I heard the forest call me like an old familiar friend, for nature truly was one of my closest companions. I answered that call and ran with such anticipation into the woods, my mind racing with the colorful characters and dreams that awaited me there.

The tree line that distinguished the manicured grass of my backyard from the untamed forest beyond it was a wonder to me. It was as if God Himself created it as the boundary line of all enchantment. As if, at that exact spot, all the world would come alive like creatures being freed from a spell. As I ventured into the woods, the carpet before me changed from the lush green of grass to the browns and golds of leaves lying all over the forest floor. The crunch of the leaves beneath my feet would rise like a melody. An occasional snapping of a twig beneath my feet also emerged like rhythm accompanying the music. And over all this melody and rhythm there was the harmony of stillness, a quietness only nature can bring. This symphony touched me deeper than any song ever could.

The fragrance of the oaks mingled with the musty smell of moss and puddles of water. My hands would reach out and touch the bark of the towering friends around me. Blacks and grays decorated the bumpy surface, which felt rough under my fingers. These soaring trees reached up into the heavens, creating a canopy of timber and leaves above my head. The light from the sky cascaded through the leaves, casting gleaming columns that stretched from floor to ceiling like pillars in an ancient temple. I would weave my way through this sanctuary, a worshiper who had reached the end of her pilgrimage. Quietly, I would settle on a moss-covered log or a palette of leaves and take in the warmth of the rays as they kissed my skin. To the untrained eye, I was all alone, for here I sat in the middle of the woods without another living soul around.

At the same time, I knew I was never there alone. Undoubtedly, these trees were my companions, these fragrances my friends. But there was a greater Friend who joined me there. These other companions were simply joining me in worship of such an acquaintance, such a Creator, such a God. I was a single note penned in a concerto as I sat next to such magnificence; so small, so miniscule in the grand scheme of the Master's symphony. And yet, this very revelation of my smallness was teaching me significance. For Almighty God spoke to me here, under these canopies of trees. I heard His voice in the whistling wind, in the sparrow's song, and even more upon my worshipping heart. I understood that every snap of a twig, every babble in the brook, was not simply creatively singing their love to God, those things were *God singing His love song to me.* There was no doubt. Here in these woods, God was teaching me to know His voice, and it was the sweetest sound I could ever know.

AND YET, THIS VERY REVELATION OF MY SMALLNESS WAS TEACHING ME MY SIGNIFICANCE. FOR ALMIGHTY GOD SPOKE TO ME HERE, UNDER THESE CANOPIES OF TREES.

It's no surprise, then, that when I started journaling and setting the eyes of my heart to see Jesus, the vision that flooded my holy imagination was that of Him clothed in a simple white garment with a red-belted sash sitting in lush green grass under a deeply rooted tree. Resting quietly under its branches, the Lord embodied a carefree contentment as He sat casually with arms relaxing on bent knees before Him, back resting on the large trunk for support. The tree was ancient in its appearance and beautiful in strength. The way the branches stretched out horizontally with delicate twists gave the tree the appearance of an old southern plantation oak tree with verdant branches dancing so low to the ground that one could easily take them by the hand and be swept into their waltz. Its trunk, too, was grand in appearance, having a girth so wide I could never wrap my arms around it. It was the perfect tree for any playful child or reflective poet, for in its branches one could easily imagine the magnificent or meditate with inspiration.

Over time, as the Lord opened my eyes to see further in this vision, I discovered that this tree was in the midst of a garden. Quietly hidden from the bustling busyness of industrial life, this garden was quaint and inviting; it had an Austen-esque feel. Ancient moss-covered stones piled one on top of another formed a low-level wall surrounding the garden, not to keep strangers out, but merely to decorate its borders. The stones were cool to the touch and beautifully married with the rolling hills for what seemed like endless miles. Nestled into the rough-hewn stone wall was a beautiful wooden door—one I did not know existed the first few times I saw the garden.

EVERY PLACE IN THIS GARDEN OF MY HEART—THE ANCIENT TREE, THE ROLLING HILLS, THE SANDY SHORE— WAS ANOTHER PULPIT, ANOTHER SCHOOLROOM.

Farther along the wall's border, just downhill from the tree, was a sapphire ocean foaming with billowing waves. The first time I saw this massive body of water, I was so surprised to see an ocean right next to billowing green hills! The shore that lined the ocean's lapping waves was one the Lord would walk along while talking with me again and again. Every place in this garden of my heart—the ancient tree, the rolling hills, the sandy shore—was another pulpit, another schoolroom. It was yet one more place the Lord would teach me His words and show me His ways. And all it took to enter this great place was the simple action of quieting my heart and setting my gaze on Him. Each time I did, I was right there in my garden—with Him.

THE DOOR IN THE GARDEN WALL

During one of my earlier journaling endeavors, I sat in stillness fixing my eyes on Him, and I found myself asking a question.

"Lord, if my heart were to have a door, what would the door of my heart look like?"

I suddenly see Jesus before me, smiling. He is wearing a long white garment that reaches to His feet. On His feet are simple brown sandals; a humble belt is around His waist. He is dressed so unassumingly that one would never notice Him simply based on His attire. That smile on His face, however, is the warmest invitation one could ever receive. As soon as you look at Him, a feeling of coming home settles in your heart. A kindness radiates from Him that says to your soul: *This is where you belong.*

Jesus gestures with His hand to His left and reveals a door: the door to my heart. I stare intently at the image before me, trying to catch every detail with my spirit's eyes. It is a heavy wooden door with planks that are old and weathered, but charming in beauty. The door is painted in a muted red color, not bright and flashy, but warm and pleasant to the eyes. It is shaped like an old church door, complete with an arched entryway with points connecting at the top as is so often seen in great cathedrals across Europe. In fact, I am certain as I stare at it that it must be the door to a very old church. There is a small window in the center board, but I cannot seem to see through it at the moment. I step closer and put my hands on the wood, drinking in the roughness of the antique architecture. Mossy stones, much like on the garden wall, encircle the door, framing it in a distinguished design. My eye is drawn down to the right of the door, where an iron handle dangles. I reach out and wrap my hand around the cool iron lever and gently twist it and push the door open. As the door slowly releases from the latch, I peek my head inside with great wonder. Looking down, I see there is a smooth stone step directly in front of the door. I reverently open the door farther and step onto that smooth stone. I cannot see too far in the distance; the eyes of my heart are unable to look that far.

Instead, I turn my attention to what is before me. There, to my left, is a hand-constructed stone wall stretching out beyond my scope of sight. Creeping ivy has made its way up the cold surface of the stone, mingling its green leaves into the mossy, craggy surface below it. I look down at the step I am standing on and find green grass growing all along the base. I close my eyes and breathe deeply, listening to the sounds of birds singing. It is in that moment I am made aware of where I am. I am in a garden, a holy garden of worship!

This thought leads me to a question that overwhelms me, and tears fill my eyes. I whisper my question to Jesus: "Oh, Lord! I am suddenly moved by a thought: is this how you see me? Is my heart this garden?"

Although unseen before me, Jesus replies to my heart, "Child, you are my garden enclosed [Song of Songs 4:12]! It is what I've promised about you! It is what I've declared over you. It is not just song or script. It is truth, dear child. You are my locked garden, the one in whom I delight, in whom is no fault or fray [Song of Songs 4:7]. You are sealed and set apart for my enjoyment. It is ours, darling of my heart. Here in this inner chamber of you, I find my rest. Why do you marvel at this? Has this not been your heart's cry? To be the resting place of the Lord [1 Corinthians 3:16]?"

I am weeping as Jesus moves my heart with His words. As I wipe my eyes, I look up and suddenly find that I can now see farther into this garden. In wonder, I stand on that stone step, eyes widening as a beautiful garden unfolds before me, a vast landscape of rolling hills, blossoming flowers, and butterflies clumsily dancing from bloom to bloom. Mouth agape, I turn to my right and see a splendorous tree downhill a ways. Underneath its branches is a park bench where Jesus is sitting, His foot resting on His opposite knee, casually smiling and relaxing in the shade. His hands are resting on His knees and His head is back, eyes closed, with that beautiful smile on His face. I stand with feet frozen taking in the scenery. Everywhere I gaze is absolute beauty. There is lush grass all around, birds flying by in the distance and above my head. I can hear the sound of a stream laughing somewhere in the distance. Right in front of me and to my left are curtains of yellow roses growing up a trellis near the garden wall. I notice for the first time that a huge oak tree is growing just outside the stone wall structure, casting its branches and shade over my left shoulder. With mouth still wide in wonder, I step off the raised stone for the first time and walk toward the roses growing up the trellis to my left just a few steps away. Along the way, I run my fingers over the rock wall, the furry moss and cool stones tickling my fingers. I reach the roses and close my eyes while drinking in the fragrance of the blooming buds.

A feeling of absolute peace fills my lungs as an awareness of His presence washes me from the inside out. Opening my eyes, I notice a tiny garden pond to my right and I have to laugh at the chubby little angel statue standing on its bank, pouring water from the pot in its chiseled hands into the pond. I chuckle at the irony of finding such a statue here of all places! Ever since I read in the Scriptures what cherubim actually look like (fearsome flames of angelic fire!), the paintings and statues of baby-faced, cupid-inspiring angels has made me scratch my head at where man came up with such an idea. I chuckle and shake my head at the humor of the thought of finding such a statue in such a sacred space. The sound of my name being called interrupts my musings; I turn my ear to listen. It is Jesus calling me from the bench under the tree.

"Child! Child, come over here!"

Eagerly I respond to His invitation. I look down and see a stone path laid out for me leading away from the pond and to the edge of the partitioned rose garden. I go from stone to stone, eyes locked on my feet with each step. Some of the stones beneath them are shaped like butterflies: colorful red, purple, and silver gems decorating their wings. Other stones are round and covered in what appear to be colorful smooth glass pieces of varying sizes and shades. Red tulips are growing along the path, and I cannot help but stop and smell them. As I do, a bee buzzes by, but I am not afraid of it. I smile and watch it clumsily fly away. I feel like a child, so much alive in this moment as I skip from stone to stone stopping to enjoy the beauty. I can hear Jesus laughing.

"You love nature!" He says.

A golden-brown bunny hops over to me and I bend down excitedly to pet its velvet fur. I look up at Jesus while I pet the creature. He is smiling, taking pleasure in the very pleasure I feel.

"Yes, Lord," I answer. A thought is exchanged without words, one of thanks for having the bunny here.

"You are welcome." Jesus smiles.

I walk over and sit next to Him on the bench. He casually places His arm around me. I sigh with the greatest contentment I have ever known. Together, we gaze up into the tree, which grows tall and reaches over our heads. My earlier thought fills my mind once again: this lovely garden I am now envisioning is the garden of my heart, the secret place cultivated through relationship with Christ. Jesus, knowing my mind, speaks of this very thing.

"Look at all the life your love has produced here, child. Because of your love and devotion for me, the birds of the air have a place to rest. This tree has a place to put its roots. You have done this in partnership with me, child. Remember, my Father is the vinedresser [John 15:1]. He tends the garden of your heart, but only as you allow him in."

"Ah, I see!" I respond. I am taking in each word, so amazed that God sees my heart as His very own garden.

"Faith has grown in you so completely, child. I do not despise the little saplings" [Song of Songs 2:13].

Suddenly, we are no longer on the bench. We are now over by a diminutive sapling growing closer to the rose garden. It is barely three feet high and no rounder than a water hose. Still, Jesus is on one knee tending the soil around it. It is rich, black earth that He works with His hands. I bend down and join my hands with His in tending the tiny tree.

"Every area of growth in your life that you tend to is precious to me, child. Do not despise the day of small beginnings. Do not grow weary in well doing [Zechariah 4:10; Galatians 6:9]. This sapling will turn into a mighty oak."

At the Lord's prompting, my eyes are drawn to the tree that casts its grand shadow over the park bench. As I consider how this grand tree began as this little sapling, Jesus continues. "Yes, the great big tree we were just sitting under began just as this sapling—years ago, tiny in faith and growth. But you heeded to it. You gave place to it and made room for it, child [Matthew 13:31, 32]. See, I spent time removing the weeds that wanted to choke it out before it ever really took off. You gave me permission, and I was able to tend to my heart's delight [John 15:1-8]."

"I know that this garden we are in symbolizes my heart," I respond. "No doubt the things growing in it, then, symbolize various things as well. So what does this little sapling represent, Lord?"

"It is new areas of faith," Jesus says. "It is I who give you faith as a gift, and it is growing [Romans 12:3]." Jesus points to the tiny tree. "Here it is! A baby in its beginning stages! But it will not take long, child, before this is raising-the-dead kind of faith! That kind which you long for. Oh, but child! Do not be distracted in the growing process. Simply allow my love to water the soil, to weed away the doubts and insecurities, to weed away the fears of putting your eyes on yourself and on others. In time, child, this will grow into a mighty oak [Isaiah 61:3]."

An image of the tiny sapling grown in full maturity, large branches filled with beautiful white flowers, catches my eye. "I see it will have blossoms!" I say with excitement.

"Yes!" Jesus responds with even more excitement than I. "It will produce fruit and fragrance, child! You are called to let the fragrance shift in the breeze [Song of Songs 1:12]. Faith is attractive. The bees will pollinate it to other trees and cause its blossoms to spread and grow. Faith is contagious!"

ON ONE SUCH DAY, I FOUND MYSELF EXTREMELY UNSURE OF MYSELF, DOUBTING IF ANYTHING I WAS SEEING OR HEARING HAD ANY "GOD" IN IT AT ALL.

"Beautiful, Lord." I smile and sigh, contentment washing over me.

Once more, the scene within my spirit's eye changes. We are now walking hand in hand away from the little sapling. The giant tree is far to our right, and the garden gate is to our backs. I feel Jesus' strong fingers gently holding mine as we swing our hands in a slight back and forth motion. I look up and am amazed to see that, somehow, in the middle of this locked garden, just beyond another garden wall, stands the ocean. I stop in my tracks and gaze out over the rolling blue waves, whitecaps foaming on the surface. We walk closer to the shore, and in a moment, we are standing on the sands, the salty breeze blowing against us. I suddenly realize how quickly we were transported here, and with wide eyes I turn and look at Jesus in amazement. He turns and looks at me, eyes widened, a playful shock forming a smile on His face. A moment of brief silence is shattered by our laughter at each other's faces and the hilarious fact of finding an ocean where I least expected it—in the middle of a garden!

"These are the waters where your faith is tested: the water of joy! This is where you come for refreshing and daring attempts to walk [Matthew 14:22-33]. Keep coming back to these waters."

And with that, the vision before me faded.

OUT ON THE WATERS

Those early days of journaling my prayers with the Lord were especially sweet. With every return to my garden I was given a new revelation of the inner workings of my heart and a new revelation of how the Father sees me. It made me excited to have vision unfold before my eyes! It made me weep as the Father revealed His nature to me. It made me laugh in one moment and sit in awed silence the next. But even in this wonder, in the early stages of my journaling, I was so unsure about what I was seeing and hearing that I was almost afraid to step out each time.

On one such day, I found myself extremely unsure of myself, doubting if anything I was seeing or hearing had any "God" in it at all. I sat down to pray and to talk to the Lord about my doubts. That's when the Lord took me to the ocean waters just beyond the walled border of the garden. By faith, I listened to His voice. I heard Him whisper . . .

"Come out on the waters."

I know I am hearing the Spirit's voice. I just know it. I close my eyes and, all at once, I see a vision of Jesus before me, Jesus standing on a moving, rolling sea in the middle of the blackest night. Although it is thick darkness all around, I can see Him clearly. He is standing there, steady and sure, hair and white garments blown by the salty night air. As usual, Jesus has a huge smile on His face and His hand is outstretched to me; He is inviting me to come near. I look down and real-ize that I too am standing on the choppy waves. With a look of sheer shock on my face, I bravely take a few steps toward Him, drawn by the sound of His gentle laughter, my knees knocking in uncertainty with each step. I am like a toddler reaching for His hand in the wobbliness of my walk.

Jesus laughs as I finally reach out and grab His hand. "Feel the unstable waves beneath your feet. Feel the splash of waves. You can do it with me!"

Eyes wide in wonder, I am barely keeping my balance as Jesus holds my hand, the feeling of my foundation moving beneath me keeping my attention locked on my feet. The sound of His playful laughter mingles with the sound of the colliding waves. Jesus slowly lets go of my hand. My face and body language communicate an uncertainty, a . . . *whoaaaaa there!* . . . but His smile replies in calm assurance. "See," He says after a moment of standing on my own. "I don't even have to steady you. Can you run on it?"

I stand on the shifting waves steadying myself, hands awk-wardly stretched before me, swaying back and forth like a junior high kid at her first dance. "I don't know, Lord," I say with hesitancy, locking my eyes on Him.

"It's OK." Jesus smiles. "Just enjoy standing. Enjoy small steps. You worry about losing your balance. If I splash and make a wave, you are worried. It's a worry with joy, in that you like the adventure, but still I ask: why? Why do you worry? I won't let you fall. There is a great lesson for you here today, child, on these waters. What do you see?"

I take my eyes off the Master and peer into the darkness. I reply, "I only see dark sky. Night all around me. And waves of ocean as far as I can see. It's just you and me out here, Lord."

Jesus seems pleased with my response. He says, "Where else

can you go?" He gestures to the vastness and nothingness surrounding us.

Wagging my head, I respond, "Nowhere without you, Lord."

Once again, Jesus takes me by the hand and leads me along on the rolling whitecapped waters. "Learning to hear me is like learning to walk on water [Matthew 14:22-33]. It's a vast ocean. It seems dark. It seems uncertain. You feel like you can make a mistake. You sure aren't ready to take off running . . . and rightly so. You are beginning your journey. But look!" Jesus releases my hand and I stand, wobbly, on the water. "You are not sinking! You are standing on what seems to be an impossible place to stand. You are overcoming one law with the greater, the natural with the supernatural. You know how to walk on dry land. But learning to walk on water is a whole new experience. But just like when you were a child learning to walk on land, you just needed one person to guide you, the encouragement of *one*.

"I feel that same joy with you now, watching you walk where you haven't walked before. You aren't afraid of the night, Beloved, because you know you are not alone [Psalm 16:7, 8]. What would be terrifying by yourself is beautiful, relaxing, and fun when it's done with me. This is the first place I'm taking you: the joyful waters of hearing God's voice. We'll stay here for a while. You will learn to trust your steps and your footing more and more. I'm in you when you cannot see me [1 Corinthians 3:16, 1 John 2:27]. You will remember this. This will be confidence in you as you take bigger steps. For now, take my hand. Feel the salty splash. Have fun. It brings me joy just watching. This is where much of my laughter comes from, child: Watching you grow. It is sheer pleasure. Oh, your trust makes my heart sing. Thank you, for your trust in me is a true gift. Trust: it fans the flame in my eye. It causes new bursts in the fire in my eyes!"

And with that, the vision on the waters faded.

THE LIFE-GIVING TREE

Day after day, the Spirit of the Lord took me back to the garden in my quiet time with Him. And day after day, without fail, He revealed things to me that were too great for my heart to come up with on its own. I knew as I leaned into what I was seeing and hearing by faith that the depths of His heart was what I was finding, and yet I also knew that what I was experiencing was just the tiniest portion of a drop of who He is! One of the deep seeds of revelation He gave me in prayer was when He spoke to me specifically about the tree where we met together—a tree I was soon to learn contained more to it than met my eye.

"I am inviting you to enter my kingdom. I am inviting you in."

As I breathe in this peace, I suddenly see myself standing right by the red garden door. I stand at the entrance to the garden of my heart, but I am not entering in. I am puzzled by this, so I wait on what the Spirit will say concerning this lack of entry on my part.

Then, ever so gently, the Holy Spirit continues. "There are places in the kingdom you have not begun to enter. There are places in my kingdom that you've never seen. You have stayed on the outside, the borders of my kingdom, but I am opening the gate to the heart of the city [Revelation 21:25]. There you will see mysteries, wonders like you've only imagined or never dreamed."

I am now drawn in past the door, walking a leisurely, satisfied pace toward the tree in the midst of the garden. As I scan the rolling lawn, I notice other trees in the garden that I have not seen before, just to my left. I stop and stare at these trees, an orchard filled with blossoming branches growing brightly colored fruits. Then, all at once, I am standing next to Jesus underneath the shade of this fertile grove.

"Here in the heart of my kingdom are apple trees, where, under the shade, you will eat and be satisfied [Song of Songs

2:2-5]," the Lord says. "The food will be warm in your tummy, satisfying to your mouth, giving strength for today and the journey ahead. It will give you pleasure in the midst of bitterness, in the midst of trying situations. You will walk with strength from this spiritual food in your belly, with a remembrance of this place in the kingdom all around you. You desire to carry this atmosphere with you at all times. I delight in this wish of your heart. This will be granted as you eat and drink in the center of this city. This is a new place. You like it. Look around. What do you see?"

I look up at the thick branches above me. I am standing under *our* tree—the one where the Lord first met with me. "These trees, Lord, are unlike any others." I peer into the luscious growth and see large birds hopping around from branch to branch, busily chirping to one another. "I can see birds of some kind living in them, but they are not like any birds I have ever seen. I cannot tell you why." I pause and ponder what I am feeling. I draw a breath and say, "Both these trees and these birds *look* like what I have seen on earth, but somehow they have a living nature different than on earth. It's as if they are more alive, more able to communicate with me than mere animals. There is an exchange between us because they are so alive!"

I look away from the branches and into my Lord's face. As usual, He is smiling as revelation floods me, His beautiful eyes sparkling with delight. His pleasure in my discovery causes me to hunger to learn more. In excitement, I peer across the garden to see what else I can discover about this place. In the distance, closer to where the rose terrace is located, I see angels in flowing white garments moving among the roses and at various places in the garden. Animatedly, I point toward them and say, "Lord! I see angels walking around this garden!" Somehow, I know without being told that these angels are here as ministers and servants. In wonder, I watch them. They are each carrying little picnic baskets over their arms, ready to serve anyone they find in the garden. I peer harder at one of the baskets wanting to know what the angels are carrying. A glimpse of golden-kissed apples just beneath the wicker lacing catches my eye. Then I notice a bottle of wine cradled among them. "Lord!" I exclaim. "I can see there are golden apples in that one's basket! And sweet wine too!" I laugh as the thought of eating such delicious fare floods my imagination. To eat a picnic provided by God's angels? What a thought!

My eyes are then drawn past the angels and past the garden wall behind them. I can see a street just beyond the wall lined with quaint buildings and stores. I cannot see what the stores offer, but I see angels coming and going from shop to shop greeting one another in a jovial manner. As I watch the vision, I am filled with a sense that I am standing in a garden park in the heart of a city, like Central Park in New York, a safe haven of rest in the midst of busy activity. I peer down the street, smiling as I watch angels greet one another as friends.

Jesus comes into view again; He is standing to my left. "This is home," He says. "This is the lovely place of my dwelling. All are called to live here, but few venture in past the gates. Notice, not many people have come here."

I look around the park and, for the first time, notice that very few people are here. Although this garden represents my heart, I know it also represents the Secret Place—the place of rest in the kingdom that all of God's children are invited to enter. I see a couple individuals on a picnic blanket over by the roses; they are enjoying the food that one ministering angel provides. Other than that, I don't see anyone in the park.

This makes me stop and wonder: *How did I get here? Is it hard to find? How do I get here again?*

Jesus replies, "Follow my invitation. Obey the little prompting of peace [John 14:25-27]. Sometimes, you will enter simply by hushing yourself. You will find this happening while pushing your grocery cart at Walmart. You will feel this hush come over your spirit. Yield to it [Isaiah 30:11]. If you weep, you weep, even if in the middle of a store. You are learning to throw your thoughts on me throughout your day. Keep doing this and you will find that you have entered into this place, this garden of my presence [Colossians 3:1, 2]. You will soon learn through practice how to remain here. You will be able to sense when you have left. You are called to remain here, to eat so that you can venture out into the world. The difference will be that you have learned to sustain yourself and constantly return to this place of possessing presence."

Jesus' words wash over me. They are so full of light it's as if darkness in my mind that I didn't even know was there is chased away with every word. I am changed each time He speaks. I look up at the abundant canopy of branches above us and then back at the Lord. A question enters my mind as I stare into His beautiful eyes. Immediately, I hear myself think, *That's a stupid question.* His words have spurred in me such confidence that I am unafraid to ask Him questions I believe are ridiculous. Timidly, I say, "You know the nagging question in my heart, Lord. Is this tree we are meeting under the Tree of Life [Genesis 2:9]?"

Without hesitation, Jesus states, "It is a tree of life—a tree that sustains *your* life. This tree, like all trees in the garden, is rooted to the same tree: *the* Tree of Life. All these trees are rooted to the one source. They are sources, types that grow from the One [Revelation 22:1, 2]."

As Jesus says this, the scripture from Revelation 22 suddenly makes sense. Funny, I had not even known that it didn't make sense to me until this very moment! The Scripture reads:

And He showed me a pure river of water of life, clear as crystal, proceeding from the throne of God and of the Lamb. In the middle of its street, <u>and</u> on either side of the river was <u>the tree of life</u>, which bore twelve fruits, each tree yielding its fruit every month.

This Scripture clearly shows that *the* Tree of Life grows in the middle of the street and on either side of the river. It is one tree with multiple trees growing from it! As this revelation floods me, the Lord continues.

"These trees, from the one, grow different fruits for different seasons. You will eat of this tree, but will one day eat of *the* tree in the center of the garden. For now, you are called to the apple tree, the place of refreshing and strength for this day [Song of Songs 2:2-5]. It is life, for it is of me, the One True Tree. It is rooted and grounded in me. It grows up from me. There are many trees for you to eat of. But you will begin here. This is one spot for you to return to. I will tell you when the season has changed [Song of Songs 2:10]. Listen to the promptings of others around you, of angels ministering to your heart in this season. You have things to learn here. Pay attention to the little things. It may be silly, it may feel odd, but you will learn and grow so much in this season of trusting. All the while, I will be right with you. You can ask questions of me at any time. There is wisdom in that, so feel free."

And with this, the vision dims.

My lessons in the garden gave me such confidence to simply keep trying to use my spiritual eyes and ears. With the words of Jesus ringing in my heart, I returned to journaling again and again, believing that, even if I didn't hear it all correctly, He was a big enough God to guide and correct as He wills. Throughout my journaling, even to this day, I will stop and say, "Lord, am I hearing correctly?" . . . "Spirit, keep me on track" . . . "Father, fill my

THE STORIES WE HAVE ABOUT JESUS IN THE BIBLE ARE MORE THAN STORIES: THEY ARE LIFE-GIVING TRUTHS ABOUT A REAL GOD WITH REAL FEELINGS WHO DESIRES A REAL RELATIONSHIP.

eyes and ears." I have no idea how much of the journaling is simply my holy imagination engaging with God and how much of it is God engaging with my holy imagination. This much I do know: when He speaks and I really *know* it's Him, I find levels of wisdom, healing, and grace that I could never come up with on my own. When He really speaks, it is much kinder, much gentler, and much more loving than I can ever work up in my imagination. This is a key in knowing you are hearing His voice. He is simply a good, good God who makes communing with Him as fun and as adventurous as walking on water.

Those early days of journaling really were all about growing in confidence in hearing His voice. I believe this is a major concern in God's heart for His people: for us to confidently believe that He speaks and we hear. He desires to see all of His children step out in faith in greater ways. But because He is a patient, tender Father, He often prods us along gently, encouraging us at our pace, breaking down fears and self-limitations along the way. He has tailor-made lessons for each of His children that will awaken greater love and faith within us. For the mechanic, He may use automobile and tinkering analogies to connect that person's heart to His. For the cowboy, dappled ponies and rodeos. For me, God knew that a garden overflowing with the glories of nature would connect my heart to His because I had learned to hear Him in the midst of such beauty as a child.

For each of us, I believe, the quickest entrance into the realm of hearing God speak is through quieting ourselves (Psalm 46:10). For me to enter into His presence I simply close my eyes and let His Holy Spirit flood my mind with the picture He wants to show me. I pause and wait, breathing deeply the atmosphere of peace and love that is always available for His children. All it takes to enter this atmosphere is quieting our minds and hearts from all other thoughts and tasks and simply placing our thoughts and our affections on God. By whispering a simple prayer, such as, "I love you, God," we are ushered into the manifest presence of the Most High God. It is this atmosphere of undistracted adoration that readily sets our heart to see Jesus in His glory.

Another important truth in approaching God is that, truly and unashamedly, we can ask questions of God at any time. He loves to answer our questions! He is patient in listening and explaining, although I have found that the *way* He answers and *what* He answers is often far distant from what I expect. If I do not understand something, however, I can always ask my God about it. He gives wisdom liberally to those who ask (James 1:5).

God's desire to commune with us is greater than our desire to commune with Him. How do we know this is true? I think the clearest way is found in the fact that He was willing to lay aside His eternal home, wrap Himself in flesh and blood, and come to live and breathe among us. The Word of God made flesh. The voice of God communing, fellowshipping, interacting with His creation day in and day out. Hebrews 1:1, 2 says, "God, who at various times and in various ways spoke in time past to the fathers by the prophets, has in these last days spoken to us by His Son." Think of that! God speaks to us through His Son, who is "the express image" of the Father (Hebrews 1:3). In the Old Testament, the Holy Spirit was not poured out on all flesh, only on select spokesmen, mainly the prophets. They were the ones who would hear from God, and they in turn would share God's words with the people. But since Jesus came, we all have access to God by faith "through our Lord Jesus Christ (Romans 5:1, 2)." We are *all* made special spokesmen for God because we are all given the Spirit of God (Ephesians 1:13). God has given all who call on His name the right to become children of God (John 1:12). So each believer is also given the opportunity as sons and daughters to have open communication with God their Father through the work of Jesus!

The main way He will do this is through His written Word. The stories we have about Jesus in the Bible are more than stories: they are life-giving truths about a real God with real feelings who desires a real relationship. The Bible teaches us about who God is: how He thinks, how He feels, and how He speaks. His Word, then, becomes the platform in understanding that He speaks in various ways to this day. For instance, in Acts 4 we find the disciples asking God to give them bold-ness to proclaim the name of Jesus in the face of persecution. How did God answer? By filling them with His Spirit and literally shaking the building (Acts 4:29-31)! In Acts 9:10, we learn God spoke to Ananias in a vision. In Acts 10:9-16, He spoke to Peter in a trance. In Acts 18:9, He spoke to Paul in a dream, and in Acts 23:11 it says Jesus literally appeared standing next to Paul to talk to him! From trances to visions to impressions to dreams, God speaks in various ways to His people by our great mediator, Jesus. He made the way for *all* of us to hear His voice!

Hebrews 2 tells us that since the Father speaks to us through Jesus, "We must give the more earnest heed to the things we have heard (Hebrews 2:1)." In context, the writer of Hebrews was encouraging weary, persecuted believers to not turn back from their faith. But I believe there is also an application here for all those hungry to grow in the knowledge of God. The lesson is simple: God speaks in various ways, so "give earnest heed" to His voice by paying attention to even the littlest prompting, even the smallest coincidence, and even the most fleeting of thoughts. Because God loves to communicate, there's a great chance He is speaking to us in these simplistic ways. So whether He leads you to a garden in your mind's eye or simply impresses a phrase on your heart, go with it. Lean into it. Ask God about it. It just might lead you into a conversation with your holy Father that leaves you forever changed.

CHAPTER CONFIDENCE KEYS: HOW TO HEAR GOD'S VOICE

1. When God speaks to you, you will find levels of wisdom, healing, and grace that one could never come up with on his or her own. When He truly speaks, it is much kinder, much gentler, and much more loving than one can ever work up in their imagination.

2. God will often speak to us in ways that match our personality

and interests. He may use poetry to speak to a poet. He may use sales analogies to speak to a salesmen. He made us each unique and will communicate with us in our uniqueness.

3. Learning to hear God can seem uncertain. So enjoy small steps of faith! Maybe you aren't ready to prophesy to someone or give them a word of knowledge, but maybe you can give a cup of water to someone who looks thirsty or simply write down your prayers for the first time. Small steps over time really add up!

4. Yield to little promptings of peace. Even if it is just for a moment, stop and take a deep breath and say, "Come, Holy Spirit." Maybe He isn't going to tell you to do a thing; maybe He's manifesting himself just so you can spend time together. Whatever the case, just yield to the peace or joy or other fruit of His Spirit you are sensing, and you will find that you are easily connected to Him.

CHAPTER CONFIDENCE KEYS: KNOWING WHO YOU ARE IN GOD

1. The Lord delights in you. He sees your heart as a beautiful place in which to dwell. He really loves you—and, yes, He really likes you too.

2. The Lord takes pleasure in the pleasure *you* feel. He loves to see you enjoy life at all kinds of levels. He wants you to know that it's OK to have fun, and He desires to connect with you in those moments.

3. The Lord is excited about every area of growth in your spirit, even the smallest. He doesn't wait to rejoice over massive milestones in your life, but rejoices in every baby step along the way. He truly enjoys watching you grow! It causes His heart to overflow with joy every time you attempt a new area of faith.

4. You are not called to "fix your heart" and make fruit grow. You are called to simply yield to the One who made you and dwells in

you, allowing His hands to have their way in the garden of your heart. He is the vinedresser and you are the vine. Yield to His work, knowing that He loves you and will produce good in you.

5. God the Father, God the Son, and God the Holy Spirit are simply good. They are so much kinder than we realize. He never wants you to be afraid to ask Him questions or approach Him with your concerns or your pleasure. He is so very good and simply wants to invite you into that goodness.

Chapter 2

LESSONS FROM
THE CROSS

One of the most important things about knowing how to hear the Holy Spirit is understanding that He will always point to Jesus. For lack of a better word, it is a "job" of His to "teach us all things and bring to our remembrance all things that Jesus has said to us" (John 14:26). Jesus also told us that the Spirit would testify of Him and take what is His and declare it to us (John 15:26, 16:13). We can rest assured, then, that the Holy Spirit will always lead us to Jesus and His Word.

Some of my favorite times in prayer are when the Spirit simply speaks to me about Jesus—not my heart, not my strength or weakness, not my circumstances. Just, and only, Jesus. Every time we commune He talks to me about His nature, but the times when He *only* speaks to me about His nature are very special discussions. It is hard to put into words except to say that in those moments I am more aware of who He is as God. And He is holy. He is awesome. He is more beautiful and more terrifying than words can tell. He is the eternal One who is coming to judge the living and the dead, the One who is a consuming fire and yet also living love. What a mystery our God is! With every revelation I receive of Him, I know it is just a fraction of a drop—a miniscule drop—of who He is. I only have two eyes to see Him. The cherubim before His throne are covered with eyes and have been studying Him since eternity's beginning and they have not ceased to say, "Holy! Holy! Holy! Lord God Almighty!" (Revelation 4:6-8). If this is what *they* see, this too is what I will see every time I come into His presence.

The Lord's holiness captures all of Heaven's attention, causing the angels to sing, but there is another endless song being lifted up in the courts as well. It's the song that Revelation 5:11, 12 says is being sung by ten thousand times ten thousand, and by thousands of thousands: "Worthy is the Lamb who was slain to receive power and riches and wisdom and strength and honor and glory and blessing!" Worthy is the Lamb who was slain! It's the song of the Lamb, of the redeeming One who has washed us in His blood. Simply put, all of Heaven is captured by the cross. How much more so, then, will the Holy Spirit direct my heart in prayer over and over again to look upon the cross of Christ? The song that the cherubim sing is directly tied to the song that the ten thousands sing and the song that the ten thousands sing is directly tied to the song that the cherubim sing! His blood cleanses us because He is holy. His holiness is what makes Him worthy to receive all honor and glory and blessing and power. But oh, the mystery that is His blood that makes us holy as He is holy.

WHAT HE DID ON THE CROSS HE DID BOTH *FOR* US AND *AS* US. THE TRUTH REMAINS: WE HAVE BEEN CRUCIFIED WITH HIM (GALATIANS 2:20).

The cross of Christ is both our beginning and our end, for here the old man died and the new life began. It is both our shame and our victory, for here our sin crucified the innocent One, but it is also here that we were made right with God.

Even more mysterious is that Calvary is both the Lord's cross and our cross. What He did on the cross He did both *for* us and *as* us. It's a deep theological truth that many scholars shy away from, or one many theologians argue about. But the truth remains: we have been crucified with him (Galatians 2:20).

Although a lot of my time with God is spent receiving His tender love and learning of His resurrection power, I also know those times when the weight of His death and His holiness falls so heavy in my heart that I am left speechless, plastered to the carpet in awesome fear. What's amazing about Him is that as we grow in friendship, He brings opposite experiences together for my enjoyment: His death and His resurrection, His terror and His goodness. It's the combination of feeling so small but so loved, so lost but so *found*—all at the same time. And it's all because of the cross.

HIDING IN HIS WOUNDS

On one occasion with the Lord, He took me on an amazing journey of describing how His wounds communicated love in a way I had never considered. Even more amazing was how He explained that I, too, would best show love in the exact same way: through my wounds. Adding layer upon layer of revelation, He began to unfold to me the power of living my "daily death to self" from within His death. It's a mystery that is best described by His Spirit in the journaling below. This is yet another proof that He speaks through a heart that is yielded in this way, for *my* words are never adequate enough to describe what He can so eloquently say in just one remark.

"Good morning, Lord. I feel you near. I love your nearness. Truly, it is our good . . . *my* good, Lord [Psalm 73:28]. That you are near is wonderful, marvelous, oh God. Thank you for being close to your creation. I feel a tug and a trouble in my heart today. I don't know what it is. You can show me, Spirit, or feel free to speak anything that's on your heart toward me or through me today. I want to hear your voice. I tune my heart now. Come, Holy Spirit."

As quickly as I wait, the Spirit of the Lord whispers to my heart, "You are beautiful to me, child. Do you know this?"

I smile, choosing to believe His words over my feelings. "I know I am worth much to you, Spirit."

"Come, sit with me a while."

With His words, I suddenly see myself sitting on a log against our tree. Jesus' hand is in mine, His palm facing upward. I see the deep nail scar in His flesh and I hear Him whisper in my ear, "This is love."

I put my fingers in the scar and tenderly feel where the nails once were. I begin to weep; I am overcome with emotions. I bury my face in His palm and let the tears fall.

"This was for me?"

"Do not weep, daughter of Zion. It is a finished work—but an unfinished love," the Lord assures me. "This love is still working in you, melting away fears and insecurities, selfish ambitions and false dreams. I am reshaping you in the palm of my hand. I hold you near. No one can take you from the palm of my hand [John 10:28]. This scar: you are nestled in. My flesh is your covering. I am your shield and your God. I guard you with my very being. You are nestled in the safest place in the world."

I look up and stare at Jesus' face. "Oh, I do believe that, Lord. Show me more."

Jesus smiles and directs my eyes again to His hand. "You are safe here, child. Look into my wounds."

As I stare at His hand, an overwhelming sense that this vision isn't just something I'm making up floods me. Suddenly, what

I am seeing seems more real than ever before, as if my eyes are seeing clearer. Shaking my head in wonder, I pronounce, "This is a real hand. Real flesh and blood."

The voice of the Lord speaks to my heart. "I am familiar with your weakness, child. I am like you [Hebrews 4:14-16]. I know you. It is time for you to know me more. I will take you there as your heart desires. I will show you new depths of love, the love that is written in my wounds [John 15:13]. There are depths to these wounds that you have yet to discover. See yourself in these caverns, in these my scars, digging for new gold. Everything you see here is yours. You have rights to discover my love and the depths hidden from the foundations of the earth. My wounds were carved from the foundations, like the canyons [Revelation 13:8]."

Jesus' words each hold a vision of what He is describing. As I gaze at the depths of His wounds, the words of a song spill out of my heart: "God, I look to you. I won't be overwhelmed. Give me vision to see things like you do."

"You are nearer to my heart than you know. Step into these wounds. You can be no closer. Hide yourself in me [Colossians 3:3]. Come away and hide yourself in me. Here I have created refuge for you, refuge from the storms of life, yes, from the cares of the world. But here, in this holy dwelling of my scars, I have prepared for you a home. Here in the tabernacle of Me, I created for you a place to dwell. Crawl inside of me and sit a while. Stay here. Make your home in me. Hide yourself in me" [John 15:4; 1 Corinthians 6:17].

His words capture my heart. But all at once, another vision comes that takes me by surprise. It seems really out of place, so I study it for a moment: it's a vision of what comes to mind whenever I read the scene about Mr. Tumnus's home built into a cave in *The Chronicles of Narnia*.

"Lord," I say quizzically, "I am seeing the cave of Mr. Tumnus from the book *The Chronicles of Narnia* for some reason. I am seeing it like I imagine it when I read the book, all warm and cozy."

I feel Jesus smile. "I am the cleft of the rock, child [Exodus 33:22]. These wounds are the cleft. You are remembering the coziness described in the book because, yes, you can come to the cleft and make a home there."

I laugh as the cozy cave vision transforms again. "Now I see a castle, though! Wow! You are both the cozy nest and the glorious home!"

Jesus chuckles. "I am *all* things that you need, child. I am your all in all. Here in my wounds, I display my love. I will never leave you alone. I will not forsake you. You will never be orphaned again. Here in my wounds I prepare the place for you. In the presence of your enemies you can feast at my table in my wounds. I am in you and you are in me. I am in you working out my love. Yes, I am working out what I have worked in you [Philippians 2:13]. You will see the fruit of it upon the earth. I am working all throughout my bride to strengthen her. I will be seen

"IF THIS IS LOVE, THESE WOUNDS IN MY HANDS AND FEET, THEN YOU MUST SHOW LOVE THROUGH THESE WOUNDS."

by my love through my people. I am working it out. These wounds are the key, the doorway into my heart and love for my people. Do not be quick to overlook the real flesh and blood of my hands. I show you this tenderly, child. I want you to partake of my wounds. I want them to be your own in that you know who they belong to and are pleased to share in them with me. Do not be afraid of my wounds. You are wondering about this. No, to you it doesn't seem that you are afraid of them. You love my death, and I know this, child. But take them as *your own*. Of this do not be afraid! Step into them more and more."

Puzzled at His explanation, I ask a single question: "How?"

"Understand what the will of the Lord is for your life," Jesus answers. "Live the life I have called *you* to live as the *living sacrifice*. Share with others the things, the gifts, the callings I have placed inside of you. Sometimes this will bring about a persecution, a wounding of the soul. Embrace it. Other times it will bring blessing. Embrace it as well. I will be with you as you rise up into that new man I am creating [Ephesians 2:15]. Let my love show through you in the smallest details. Understand every cup of cold water is grace given [Matthew 10:42]. It is love shown. You must display my love through the wounds. Let others see them in your life. If this is love, these wounds in my hands and feet, then you must show love through these wounds."

I sit pondering Jesus' words. I mull them over and unpack each one. Slowly, I respond, "I must be 'more of you and less of me.' I understand this prayer of John's so much more [John 3:30]. Oh, this mystery! I need your grace to understand it."

Jesus says, "You no longer live. You must remember that. Even in your day-to-day activities, be sure you realize it is not you who are called to live, but you are called to die [Galatians 2:20]. I am called to live in you and through you. Let me be your eyes and your ears, your voice and your touch. I will see what you cannot see and do what you cannot do. This is a lesson you are learning. Do not slip away from it, child. Stay anchored to it. It can be overwhelming for those who do not keep their eyes on me. Be sure you look to me through this season of learning and testing. Let me guide you into the right path and destiny. Do not fear the change that is coming. Hold tight to me. I will guide you through. You will not see far enough ahead to know the next step, but I will. Hold tight to me and to the work that I have begun and will finish in you."

I smile. "You are my light, Jesus." With this, I smell—strangely—a whiff of overheating electrical equipment! I open my eyes and look around the room where I am seated. I get up and touch the outlets, cords, and other electrical objects in the room, sniffing for any sign that something is overheating. I find nothing.

I settle back down to talk to the Lord and close my eyes. As soon as I do, I smell the same thing. "Lord, there it is again. Is this you talking to me [Hebrews 5:14]?"

His Spirit speaks to me. "When too much power is going through the board or object, it will overheat and cause that acidic kind of smell. The current must match the vessel in size and power. The current of electricity must match the size of the individual that holds it."

I marvel and smile. The way He speaks . . . even through it is just a fragrance, it is simply amazing. All I had to do was ask Him about it and He was quick to teach me. Cocking my head in wonder, I reply to my Teacher, "By myself I have a certain level of power. But in you I have all the power I need?"

I feel His smile as He responds. "Love is power, child. My Spirit flowing though you in love is power. Soulish love will cause you to overwork and overheat. Agape love—living, pulsating, breathing love—can only flow through those who have died on the cross, who have hung it all out there, who have said 'Yes, Lord' to my ways and my calling. Yes, this is the will of God for your life. Let my power work through you. It will come through love. It is the purest form of power on the planet. I will still work through you in power outside of love, but it will always lead to overheating. In other words, I will still flow through you in power when you pray for people or preach a sermon, but apart from love, you will overheat. But for those who carry the power with love until their dying day, these are the ones whose vessel will match the flow of power. Live in me and through me—live in *my vessel*, my wounds—and you will always have power and love working together."

And with this, my vision faded.

THE FELLOWSHIP OF SUFFERING

I can confidently say that some of the deepest times with the Lord are when He reveals the beauty of His death to me. The depths of love that His cross speaks are endless. The glory that His death provides is unfathomable. And yet, for all its beauty, I must remember that His death was utterly agonizing for Him. He was a real person enduring real, unimaginable pain.

During one time in prayer, He invited me to understand the "realness" of the things He suffered that day on Calvary, and with this invitation, my heart was forever changed.

"Jesus, thank you for being the servant, the very one Isaiah said would come [Isaiah 52:13 through Isaiah 53]. I am amazed at the accuracy of the prophecies! How you fulfilled them, Lord! Oh, thank you that you came with the Spirit of God upon you. Thank you that you walked in wisdom and knowledge of things too great for us to understand. Thank you that you were willing to be humbled, humiliated, ridiculed, and beaten to the point of being unrecognizable. It's cruel. I am sorry for you and yet so thankful to you. I believe you have brought me freedom from my prison! You have opened my eyes! Beloved! I love you. Thank you for being all that Isaiah said you would be and more. What would you like to say to me in light of all of these promises? How should I respond to you today?"

As I wait on him, I hear the Lord say, "Look upon my cross."

A dark image of the feet of Jesus nailed to the cross fills my vision. Although there is darkness all around, I can see that His legs and feet are soaking in blood. The picture is so disturbing, for I know I am the one who did this to Him. An overwhelming feeling of the cost He paid because of me weighs upon me. Crying, I say, "In so many ways, Lord, it reminds me of my unworthiness, that my sin did this to you."

With the image still before me, I hear the Lord speak. "This is the sorrow of the cross, the penalty of sin: that the Righteous died for the unrighteous [Romans 5:8]. It is true sorrow, child. But it does not show your unworthiness—it shows my worthiness. It shows my victory over sin. All of your shame is conquered by my powerful display. To know the fellowship of my suffering, child, begins when you see yourself as the one for whom I died. Seeing yourself like this raises many responses in the human heart: sorrow, distress, depression, discouragement. This is the weight of sin that you feel. It depresses mankind, pushes them low into the dirt, the dirt symbolizing the nature of self and sin, like the father of sin crawling on his belly in the dust [Genesis 3:14]. Yet I am the One who made man out of the dust. I redeem even the dust! I redeem all of the earth! All of the earth in you is redeemed! It is purchased back with my most precious blood! You are no longer unworthy dirt. You are worthy! You are holy dirt, holy earth! You are set apart for divine purposes."

I let His truth wash over me, lifting the feeling of depression at such a sight as the cross. I am in no hurry. I wait until my heart connects with the glory of His words. When I feel that I am truly receiving His peace, I ask, "Tell me more about the fellowship of sufferings, Lord" [Philippians 3:10].

"To know me is to know my pain, child," Jesus continues. "It is to see the grief in my eyes. The onslaught of venom that was attacking me that day was unbearable in my own human strength. The blows cut deep in a way you will never understand. The pain of heartache was too great to bear. I looked for my closest friends and found none [Matthew 26:31-55]. Only a few hung by in my darkest hour. I was so low. So lonely. So broken. Yet, in my heart I knew my hope—you . . . and all mankind [Hebrews 12:1, 2]. In my Father's strength I saw my reward. I saw the great day when I will gather all of my people back to my Father's heart, back into His family, back to the day as it was in the beginning where you once walked and talked with my Father and me, where my Spirit ran playfully among you and there was no fear. I saw this day ahead of me.

I saw you. I knew your name and I knew it was worth it all.

"My suffering led to this freedom. Suffering is not always bad, you see, child. Even what you suffer here on earth at times is direct from my hand. This is hard for man to fully grasp. *Suffering is to know me.* It is to find me in a special way. When you come to the cross and take it as your own, you will find suffering. The first kind of suffering you find is that unworthy feeling—the pang of the heart toward me and my price. But if you press on through this, you will find joy unspeakable and full of glory [1 Peter 1:6-9]! You will find peace for your journey. The cross offends many. The price of it, the stench of it, how it reveals the wickedness of the human heart, drives many to recoil from its personage. They look at it and say, 'I do not want to think of myself as lowly and wicked! I am good on my own!' And they turn away from me. But for those who will humble themselves, bearing the weight of mild suffering within themselves, wrestling with the fact that they are separated from God's holy nature, those who will do this *and* press on through the cross, they will find resurrection power. That which was death gives way to life. Many preach this yet do not walk in it. I first call you to the cross. It is true. But I will always lead you to life. If you know the fellowship of my sufferings, I *will* call you to the fellowship of my life and resurrection. I will call you higher if you go lower [1 Peter 5:5, 6]. When trials come your way, child, do not look quickly for the escape. Look to me!"

I sense a smile and warmth in this statement, and although I am not seeing anything but the image of the cross, I know that Jesus is near me smiling. It seems a strange time to be smiling, however, since He is speaking of trials coming my way! With joy in His voice, He says, "You see, I will allow certain trials to come through my hands—always filtered—to test you, not in a hard way or a mean way. No, I simply show you what you are really made of. I see in you the purest gold. I will cause it to rise to the top in the fire of trial. I work out impurities in you in this way."

I pause and think on what He has said. I am filled with uncertainty, so I ask, "Lord, this may be stupid, but I have a question. You suffered trial and yet you did not need to be tested, for you were perfect. If suffering is to simply test and refine us, how does this apply to your suffering?"

"Ah, but I did need to be tested, child," Jesus says, "for *every* child of God is tested in this life so that in the next they can reign without exception" [Hebrews 2:10, 5:7; 2 Corinthians 4:17].

I truly did not understand His answer. Jesus needed to be tested? This seemed too bizarre. "Lord? Explain," I ask.

He gladly shares. "I was tested in every way that you are tested to show you the better way, to show you what the human heart can do when it is crucified to its own ways and alive to God's ways. I showed you how to live from day one. From the moment my feet hit the ground, till they were crucified on the tree, till they were taken up in glory—I showed you that life is meant to be lived victoriously even in the trials of life and time. God allowed me to be broken. He allowed it for your good and for mine."

Once again, I am confused, not fully grasping His answer. "How could it be for your good?" I question. "You never sinned. You had nothing to be worked out in you."

"No, I was the righteous servant who had never done any wrong [2 Corinthians 5:21]," Jesus says matter-of-factly. "But I was crushed for my own good, too, not because of disobedience, but to bring me great reward [Isaiah 53:12]. Sometimes trials have nothing to do with sin. When trials are a result of sin, it is called sowing and reaping, child. If you sow sin, you reap sin. However, when life brings you trials apart from reaping of sin, rejoice! It is a chance for your reward to be multiplied, to show the world that you are steadfast in the hour of obedience."

At this, I see a vision of Jesus resolute before His accusers at

His trial, standing unmoved as they hurl insults and accusations at Him. His face is soft but like steel at the same time, a contrasting mixture of perfect pity for His accusers and perfect obedience for His God. Beating him, ripping out His beard, and sentencing Him to death, I see that He was resolute all the way to the cross.

The Savior speaks again. "When I said yes to the Father's will for me, I laid my life down on the cross in order that I could take it up again in victory."

At once I understood what He was teaching: He could not have had resurrection life or given resurrection life if He had not gone through this trial. The trial of the cross was all about reward.

Jesus continued. "Yes, the only way I could know resurrection victory was to lay my life down on the cross. I had to die in order to know everlasting, resurrected life. I am King, eternal, forever victorious because . . . yes, I am God. But as man? It is because I laid my life down in the crucible of fire, because in that great moment of trial for my soul I laid my life down in order that I might take it up again [John 10:17, 18]. It is because of this that I gained a kingdom, because I went through the fire. Do you see? It was for my own good, too, that I laid it down. The suffering of my soul produced many sons in glory [Hebrews 2:10]! It was worth it!"

"I see it, Jesus." Weeping, I whisper, "The cross was for my good—it brought me to you. The cross was for your good—it gave way to resurrection, where you are seated at the right hand of God!"

"And where you are seated too!" [Ephesians 2:6], Jesus reminds me.

"Yes, Lord. Thank you," I reply through salty, tear-covered lips. I am overcome by His cross.

With love dripping on His words, Jesus says, "You are welcome, child. Welcome to come and feast on my resurrection life here before the throne, day and night, night and day. You are invited to the great banqueting table, where my banner over you is always love—every day, every night, forever and ever [Song of Songs 2:4]. The way to the throne life, though, begins at the cross. In your day-to-day life, you pick up your cross by embracing little areas of obedience. Pay attention to the little details of the heart."

"Like?"

"Simply responding in love and kindness when you don't feel like it," He replies, almost casually. "Even picking up the house in an attitude of surrender. All of these little areas of obedience give birth to power in your life. It's not just the prayer and the devotion time we spend together that give way to resurrection life, it's the obedience of your heart toward me in your day-to-day routine.

"This is a new concept for you, I know. You think of walking in greater power as only coming through prayer and fasting, sitting at my feet. But I'm telling you, Mary and Martha will be joined into one body. You are called to sit at my feet. This is the important part. But Martha's job is needed after the sitting has taken place. Martha should never outweigh Mary. Workers should never outweigh the lovers. However, your love *will* produce work [James 2:18]. In your life, you are growing in power when you set your heart on me in the little things of life. The serving. The seeking. The obeying. It's all hidden in the heart throughout your day. Make it your habit to sit before me all day. Bring your heart before me as you do the dishes, as you sing your songs, as you wait on tables. This is the heart of a deaconess!"

His words wash my heart, encouraging me to keep serving Him in simple, obedient love. "Yes, Lord. This is following your example."

"Yes. This is staying connected to the vine. Abiding."

His words seal my time with Him in a pleasant way. "Yes. Abiding," I reply. Abiding. This is the prayer of my heart: to simply abide all day long, just like Jesus did, always looking to His glorious cross.

THE RUTTED PATH

The Lord has called us all to take up our own cross and embrace a life of suffering for our Savior. But many things within us, and many things without, fight against the necessity of dying to ourselves. The Lord graciously explained to me in this particular journaling that very few believers ever fully embrace their own cross, but for those who will, they find a deeper union with Christ, a union that intertwines their heart with His at a sacred level.

On another day of prayer, the Lord was challenging me to take up my cross by wooing me to the glory that the cross brings—the glory of knowing Him in greater measure.

"Good morning, Lord Jesus. How I love you! I would love to talk to you about the subject I've been wanting to talk about, if this is the morning. I'd like to hear your take on the subject of me taking up my cross [Matthew 16:24-26], of walking the narrow road that is just wide enough for a cross and how, still, your burden is rest. I know there is much here by way of you, Holy Spirit. Come and enlighten my mind."

I hear the Spirit whisper on my heart, "I have been waiting." I smile.

Suddenly, I see Jesus is waiting beside our tree, leaning His left shoulder on the trunk, one foot kicked behind the other, patiently resting with a basket of apples in hand. I approach him and chuckle, saying, "You brought apples this morning!"

"Yes!" Jesus smiles. "Take and eat what I offer you, child." I reach into the wicker basket and choose a beautiful red apple as my own. I bite into the fruit and juices run down my chin.

My eyes grow large as the sticky sweetness takes me by surprise. The Lord smiles at me, kind eyes shining, and says, "Let the juice be refreshing to your taste [Song of Songs 2:3]." He pauses as I enjoy my treat, then addresses the question at hand. "You want to know about the narrow road [Matthew 7:13, 14]?"

At His words, I am no longer standing with Him under the canopy of our tree. We are now walking together under the warmth of a noonday sun along a long, narrow dirt road that seems to stretch on and on, almost endlessly. In the middle of the brown, dusty road is a deep rut carved into the earth. Somehow, I just know this rut was formed by someone carrying a cross on their shoulder, dragging the weight of it behind them. The emotion that this thought stirs inside me makes me stop in my tracks: someone has walked this road with the heaviest of burdens. Jesus pauses beside me, to my left, and watches as I reverently bend down and touch the dusty earth in the hollowed path.

The Lord, with an almost reverent stillness, explains, "This dust represents the earth, child, the fallen plane in which you must walk from here." Jesus points to the path: "to there." He then points toward Heaven. "The earth is fine and dry," He says, bending beside me, taking a handful of arid dirt in His hand. He unfolds His fingers and lets the hot wind blow the dust from His palm. "Yes, walking on the earth will cause each man and woman to thirst. The difference in each person is what they will thirst for. This is why I said you are blessed *if* you thirst for righteousness, *if* your hunger for it far outweighs what the world will offer you along the wide path [Matthew 5:6]." Jesus stands and brushes off His hands. Once again, we walk together as He continues to teach. "When you are walking this narrow way, child, and temptation comes at you, it is being echoed from the wide path." Jesus puts His right arm around my shoulder and, with His other arm, gestures all around us. "Everything else on this earthly plane is the wide path, child. Yes, those who walk it have the entire world at their disposal, but the end leads to death [Mark 8:36], for the end does not lead *out* of the earth. It does not lead home, the home you were created to dwell in. See how wide the narrow path is?"

I stop and look down at the path I am standing on and wonder at the irony of His words. "Wide" cannot come close to describing this path. I reply: "It is not very wide at all, Lord. In fact, I am taller than it is wide, and I am only 5 feet tall."

With an arm still around me, Jesus continues to lead us on the path. "It is narrow indeed," He says, "and few will find it, did I not say [Matthew 7:14]?"

"Yes." This truth saddens my heart.

"That is because this path *does* limit your options, child." The Lord pauses and turns toward me to explain. "Here there is only room for one—one desire, one Lord, one fire, one baptism, one body [Ephesians 4:4-6]. Unity and union are the way of this walk, but man's heart is to divide time and time again. But here?" He gestures to the path once more. "This is the union walk. The narrow path is so narrow that it will force you to unite. To stay on its journey, you must walk as one [Romans 13:14]."

"THE CROSS IS ALWAYS A SYMBOL OF LIFE IN MY PLAN. THERE IS DEEPER UNION FOR THOSE WHO TAKE IT UP."

"I like that, Lord. Very interesting."

"And you are right about this rut," the Lord continues as we begin to walk again. "It is formed by the cross. It is the way of the cross, for union with me cannot come any other way. Union with me must come by way of my cross [Galatians 2:20]. The cross must become your own. The fellowship of my suffering is the way to my heart [Philippians 3:10]. Oh, you can still know me and be on your way to Heaven—see, there are individual paths where there is no rut." At His words, an image of a narrow road without a rut flashes before me. I understand that some believers walk such a narrow road. I know in my heart that these are Christians who have chosen to avoid suffering and trial, to avoid the process of dying to themselves. I suddenly realize: the rut in this path isn't Christ's cross. It's the disciple's cross (Matthew 16:24-26).

"But see here?" Jesus breaks in, pointing to the dusty, rutted path we are standing on. "This path with the rut starts at *this* point: where *you* take up the cross. Here, this one chose to take up their cross so they could have *part* of me, not just follow me [Romans 6:5; John 6:56]. To have *part* of me is to unite with me, to be one with me in all things. Do you want to follow or do you want to die and be united [Hebrews 6:1; 2 Timothy 2:11]? This is the deeper walk. But the mystery that you have asked and hinted at this morning is that it is the way of true rest. Usually those who are merely following will have less rest in me because those who have taken up the cross and really take up its work in their own life find true life, true rest, true joy . . . because the war is over. The flesh is dead [Romans 6:2, 5-7].

"There is no turning back for a dead man. There is no emotional upheaval or pain in the back from carrying a burden. There is only life, only rest. My burden *is* light, child. You will come to me if you are heavy-laden and you will find rest, but that rest comes in the form of a cross [Matthew 11:28-30, 16:24]. It *is* my yoke. The narrow road *is* my walk, it is my teaching, it is my life. My yoke is easy. Dying to yourself may not seem easy in the natural. But in the supernatural, you see there is no other choice, no other option, as you are awakened to life [Galatians 2:20]. How hard is it to choose life when it is presented? Not hard at all! Yet many do not know that this is what the narrow way of suffering will lead to. They have believed the lie that it must be difficult, that it must be burdensome, not knowing that I myself said my burden is *light* [1 John 5:3]. It is easy. But it is only easy because this cross, this path, forces you into union with me.

"You see, as you walk this road, I walk with you. I pour out oil and I pour out wine [Luke 10:33, 34]. I sup with you and you sup with me. I enter into you and you enter into me, and there is nothing that can separate us. No scheme of man or evil plan can separate what God has joined together. There is a joy in the dying. There is a joy in the taking up of the cross for each day. For the one who has joy in this, they know that it means only greater union with their Savior and Master. This is the way of the cross, child—the easier way. I see you question this, for you know the choice is harder. But, child, only for those who fear man, who fear that path. It is for *joy* set before us [Hebrews 12:2]. Joy is an easy choice. Do you see this?"

Confused, I furrow my brow and look into the Savior's face. "Yes," I say, slowly. "But it's still death. And isn't that a harder choice?"

Gently, the Lord instructs. "This path is only hard for those who refuse to see its value or who are blinded to its worth. And I'm talking about the path with the rut, the union path. The One Way path. Those who fear giving up control, having to let go, those are the ones who fear dying. But you? My child, if you taste and see that I am good [Psalm 34:8], that I am meek, that I give you rest, then you will gladly lay it down, right?"

"Yes, Lord." I think about the choice to walk in union with the Lord by way of taking up His cross as my own. I look again at the rut carved into the path beneath my feet. "Oh, how I love the image of the deep rut in the road," I sigh, then wonder aloud. "It is a place of maturity beginning, isn't it?"

"Ah, yes," Jesus answers with brows raised. "Look and see all over: people growing weary on their walk here." At His words, I see an image of believers walking their individual path of salvation with shoulders slouching, feet barely moving. Some even have hot tears streaming down their weary faces. Others seem completely frustrated. Most seem as if they could throw in the towel any moment.

The Lord continues. "They have chosen the narrow path. They have chosen to follow. And great is their reward for choosing [Psalm 19:11]. But there comes a place in many of their lives, when they come face to face with the truth of their own cross: that I didn't simply die in their place." I know as He speaks that these weary believers I see are fighting against their "personal" cross. Some are facing trials and are angry that they are in pain, kicking against the refining process. Some are refusing to deny their own rights, feeling justified for such behavior as pride and arrogance. All the while, if these dear ones would just humble themselves and embrace the cross of suffering, they would find true rest.

The Lord looks over these beloved ones with a concerned gaze. These are His brothers and sisters. Truly they are, and yet He knows there is a greater depth of maturity for them if they will but take His cross as their very own. The reality is here—it is already accomplished. They must simply die to their own ideas of "neat Christianity" and take the cup of suffering. The Lord looks at me and says, "I died for them, and they are dead with me [Romans 6:8; Galatians 2:20]. This realization—that you are dead *with me*—is the beginning, the entering into union. This comes only to those who desire to know me deeper. The cry to know me deeper will lead you to a cross: a personal cross. But do not think of it as negative. Think of it as great! For look at what my cross accomplished! It is the same for you, child. When you choose this 'light' bur-den, which is easy and which gives you rest, it only brings life [Matthew 7:14]. The cross is always a symbol of life in my plan. There is deeper union for those who take it up. There is a melding together as they continue to walk into union with me. There is a greater glory because there is greater union because there is less of you and more of me [John 3:30]. Do you see this?"

Astonished, I say, "It's a great equation! I want to see it . . . really see it, Jesus. Thank you for sharing. I must stop and get ready for my day. I ask to return here to the deep rutted path, Lord."

I hear him say, "Of course. Walk with me on it today."

"OK! I love you!"

"And I love you."

IF I AM EVER HAVING TROUBLE CONNECTING WITH THE LORD IN WORSHIP, IN PRAYER, OR IN JOURNALING, ALL I NEED TO DO IS RETURN TO THE CROSS.

If I am ever having trouble connecting with the Lord in worship, in prayer, or in journaling, all I need to do is return to the cross. It is the starting place. It is the rock. It is the place of cleansing, of restoring, of adoption. The cross is the bridge that connected man back to God. Returning to the cross daily is the best prescription I can give on how to connect one's ears to the voice of the Lord. For no other word speaks louder than the blood of Jesus (Hebrews 12:24). It is the clearest communication we will ever receive on the goodness of God, the love of God, the severity of God, the faithfulness of God, the justice of God. What the cross speaks to us is an endless conversation on God's nature. Mike Bickle says of Christ's cross in his teaching on the Song of Solomon: "The most obedient and worshipful saints think the most on the cross. It is their constant meditation and confession. We will never grow weary of meditating on it."[2] If we never receive another impression from the Spirit, another word of knowledge, another prophetic vision, we have enough to listen to in the greatest proclamation God ever gave us: the cross.

In all our communing with God, the cross will always be the clearest conversation God gives us. It speaks of His love and it speaks of His wrath. It speaks of His goodness and it speaks of His holiness. It speaks of the wickedness of sin and the righteousness of Jesus. It declares His justice and His mercy. It unites the prophetic past with the promised future. The cross is central to all of history and central to all of our hearing. To paraphrase a song by David Ruis: if we never receive another promise, another healing, or another vision, the cross of Christ is proof enough that God is good.[3] Let this be the final word to all conversations: the cross of Christ is the goodness of God.

CHAPTER CONFIDENCE KEYS: HOW TO HEAR GOD'S VOICE

1. The Holy Spirit will always point you to Jesus. This is one way to know if what you are hearing is on track: does it glorify Jesus? Does it magnify His cross, His resurrection, His work, His worth? In contrast, the Holy Spirit will never glorify sin or self. He will never leave you hopeless or self-focused. All glory belongs to Jesus, and the Holy Spirit loves to give Him glory!

2. Focus on the cross. Start your prayer time there, ponder it throughout your day, revel in its power, and give God praise for it! Return to it again and again, especially when you are having a difficult time connecting with Him. If, while pondering His cross, He reveals sin in your life, confess it and know that He will cleanse you *and* empower you to be free from that sin. He is for you. The cross is proof.

3. Take up your cross by embracing little areas of obedience. The smallest things, when done as worship, matter a great deal in our maturing process. If you want hear God more clearly, obey in the smallest details of life.

4. Ask the Lord for greater union with Him by allowing Him to teach you about the narrow way. Ask for revelation about the cup of suffering, the personal cross we each must bear, and how He uses it to make us more like Him. Don't waste your trials; instead, mature in them.

CHAPTER CONFIDENCE KEYS: KNOWING WHO YOU ARE IN GOD

1. God says that you were worth dying for. You. This is personal. He had His mind on you when He counted the cost and the great reward of His suffering. You were the joy set before Him. Begin to see the cross as more than just a place where Jesus paid for your sin. Begin to see it as the place that proved how valuable you are to Him.

2. Jesus wants such an intimate relationship with you that He invites you into His darkest hour: the cross. He invites you to know Him at His most vulnerable moment and to fellowship and participate with Him there. This is friendship at the deepest level. By offering you the cup of suffering He is inviting you into the greatest reunion we can ever know.

3. The Lord sees in you the work of His cross. He sees you as holy. He sees you as righteous. He is able, then, to pull out of your spirit what you don't even know is possible. Often, it is the testing and trials of life that draw out the spiritual gold in us. There is more to you than meets the eye: let every God-filtered trial bring you into greater confidence.

Chapter 3

LESSONS FROM THE CHILDLIKE HEART

The things I was hearing and seeing in my prayer time were leaving me in awe. This casual approach to conversing with God was awakening my heart to love Him more! Time and again in those first days of journaling, I was taken by surprise at the weight of the words He spoke. I was also taken back by the vision I was seeing. Although it was all so new and sometimes so strange, I chose to press in by faith to what was being painted on my spirit's imagination. Everything, however, in my rational, religious mind warred against such creative communion. Here, in this place of prayer, there were no walls. Here there were no rules. It was just simple conversation and great leaps of faith in my fellowship with the Spirit. As is often the case when freedom first finds us, I wanted to crawl back into my safe cage of religious piety where rules and regulations kept me from becoming too fruity and weird. But I kept pursuing this new style of communion, sometimes cringing in my sensible self, determined to trust that He would not lead me where He did not go.

IT WAS SO STRIKING TO SEE MYSELF LIKE THIS: VULNERABLE, TRUSTING, OVERFLOWING WITH JOY, LEANING ON MY MAKER'S ARMS.

Maybe it was because of all the religion the Lord needed to break off of me, or maybe it was simply because of His fathering heart, but the vision I was seeing of myself with the Lord by our tree was often that of me as a little girl. It was so striking to see myself like this: vulnerable, trusting, overflowing with joy, leaning on my Maker's arms. This image of me as a child would be a lesson itself, one the Lord would take me back to over and over as He disrobed my religious, grown-up garbs and clothed me in true glory.

My lessons in becoming like a child were ones that were so powerful; the images of what I saw in prayer are forever in my heart. Truly we must have faith like a child to even believe we are communing with an invisible God (Matthew 18:1-5; Hebrews 11:6)! This is what Adam and Eve had in the garden before Satan cast his shadows of doubt: simple childlike trust. They knew their Father. They knew He was good. They had casually communed with Him. It's only when they began to question if they were hearing Him and if they really knew His heart that they found themselves naked and afraid. This lesson of maturing into childlike faith and joy is one of such importance that the Lord returned me to the garden to instruct me in its truth again and again—and still does to this day.

LEARNING TO PLAY IN PAPA'S PRESENCE

The Lord desires that I, as His child, have complete faith in who He is. That complete faith, as I was about to learn, is one that doesn't always look like what I expect it to look like. For childlike faith is far from dignified to the outward observer. But at the heart level, childlike faith is the grandest display of faith we can possess, for it is a faith that looks the impossible in the eye and never bats an eyelash.

"Good morning, Lord!" I say as I close my eyes and wait to hear Him speak.

"Good morning, child," the Lord replies to my heart. He is unseen in my mind's eye, but His words are clearly impressed on my heart. I smile at His greeting. It had come so easily. By faith? Most certainly. And yet I knew He really was greeting me this morning.

I see Jesus and me sitting under our tree. Jesus appears in His usual form: simple white robe reaching down to His sandaled feet, waist girded with a simple brown leather belt. His usual demeanor graces His face: a peace that passes understanding and a love that is completely personified in His gaze. He is His usual gloriously approachable self.

Only I am different, for in this vision I am not my current age—I am six or seven years old! Long brown curls fall down my back, tied back away from my face with a big red silk bow. I smile as I envision the little girl version of myself sitting next to my Maker. As I look with eyes of faith, I see that I'm putting bright flowers in His hair and He in mine, playfully laughing and having a wonderful time. As I stare at this image, I cannot help but chuckle and shake my head in wonder at the ever-merry, laid-back nature of Christ.

"Well, what do you want from me this morning? What can I do for you?" Jesus asks while placing a tiny daisy behind my ear.

"I should be asking you that!" I reply in a bit of shock.

Jesus laughs at my response. Leaning in toward me with eyebrows raised, He says, "Child, how about we ask each other together? Like, on the count of three?"

His lighthearted, fatherly response just amazes me. "Lord, I've never been so playful with you before!" Jesus smiles back at me. My religious, responsible side tries to get my attention, but I am filled with a confidence while staring at His beautiful smile. Sighing in pleasure, I say, "OK! Let's do it!"

Looking at one another in smiling anticipation, we say collectively, and deliberately, "One, two, three . . . " Then we rattle off as fast as we can, "What can I do for you this morning?!"

Immediately, we crack up laughing and I tumble into Jesus' arms. Our laughter subsides with a satisfied sigh. He holds me in His arms as we stare up at my tree.

"What you do for me, I do for you, child. This, right here, is enough."

I smile as I realize Jesus wants the same thing I want. Quietly, I say, "Time together."

Jesus bends His head down, still holding me in His arms, and kisses me, once again just like a father, on the forehead. Tears begin to stream down my face as I am enveloped in such love, such powerful simplicity.

After a few moments of soaking up His love, I find the strength to say, "You want what I want!"

Jesus instructs me as any father would, holding his child while teaching them truth. "The desire deep within you to know me fully and completely is my desire hidden in you. I long to be in constant communion and communication with you. I know all about you! But that desire in you, to know me more, is a desire for my presence. To be with me where I am [John 17:20-26]."

"Yes, Lord."

"Now, multiply that desire like the stars!"

With His arms still around me, I look up and suddenly the sky is night above us. The velvety blackness is filled with countless, brilliant stars.

"*This* is how I long to be with you!" the Lord whispers. "Your desire for me is but one little star. I long to be with you day after day, moment after moment, so much more than you can ever dare to dream. My love for you is greater. It exceeds all of these stars, goes way beyond eternity, time, or space [Psalm 36:6]."

Once again, His words make my heart feel so alive. I am left speechless. I feel His arms wrapped around me, and I stare up at the stars. A feeling of belonging, a feeling of being home, fills my soul, as the warmest emotions of childhood fill me.

Images of me playing and running and laughing as a little girl flash before my eyes, and I somehow know: *this* is what I am created to be like in His presence. "Jesus, I've never felt so childlike in my journaling. All I feel is fun! Joy! And yet, tears are streaming down my face, because . . . well . . . you make me clean. This feeling right here is just . . . *clean.*"

JESUS LAUGHS AND SMILES IN GRAND APPROVAL, CLAPPING HIS HANDS TOGETHER. "YES, LIKE THAT, DAUGHTER! YOU DID WELL!"

The Lord answers; He speaks directly to my heart. "There is much to be said about the purity of children. Childlike faith is pure faith. Purity will always give you a sense of cleanness and innocence. Blessed are the pure in heart for they shall see God [Matthew 5:8]. And remember what I said?" Jesus sits me on His lap and looks me in the eye. "The little children's angels always see the face of God [Matthew 18:10]? I want to restore innocence to you, child. I desire for you to be this comfortable with me all day long. When my Spirit says play, I want you to play [Ecclesiastes 3:1-8]!"

A mischievous smile spreads across my face. "Like this?" I grin.

I leap from Jesus' lap and run out onto the grass before us. I start running and jumping and twirling for Him. I am a child putting on a show for her Father, with a heart that says, "Look at me!"

Jesus laughs and smiles in grand approval, clapping His hands together. "Yes, like that, daughter! You did well!"

I run full force back toward Him and throw myself in His arms. Once again, He squeezes me tight and holds me close to His chest, gently rocking back and forth.

"You are created with a childlike heart," He says. "It is a precious gift. One that the enemy and time and circumstances will try to squelch. Every human begins with it. It is the truly wise who *keep it* all their days [Luke 10:21]. Children can play in the presence of their father even in the midst of war and destruction."

At these words, the pleasant vision of us sitting under a tree vanishes. I am now standing on a cobblestone street in the heart of a Warsaw ghetto in World War II. All around are war-torn buildings, hollowed out, ransacked shops that are mere shells of former glorious days. The gray skies above mirror the hopelessness that fills the neighborhood. I look around and feel the despair permeating my being.

And then, an unexpected sound fills my ears: the sound of laughter. I look ahead of me on the stone street and see a group of Jewish children playing with a tattered ball. Here, in the midst of great destruction, Jewish children mingle the sound of their laughter with the sound of bombs in the distance.

I am stunned at the vision before me—shocked at how children could have any joy at all in such circumstances. I drink in the image of their play in contrast with the pain all around. "Wow. They really are resilient," I say soberly, tears spilling from my eyes.

The Lord, standing beside me now, responds with a simple

"Yes."

The Lord then leads me away from the cobblestone street and through the door of one of the little houses lining the street. We walk through the open door and enter the barrenness of this two-room home. The floors and walls are free from any color or decoration. All that is present in this first room is a tiny, rusty potbelly stove; one metal pan represents the entire cookware available. There is also a rudimentary wooden table with two simple chairs pushed underneath. The next room isn't really a separate room at all. It is simply divided by a curtain. Moth-eaten blankets, threadbare and worn, are thrown onto the floors, feather pillows, tattered and torn, on top of them. This humble sight makes up the bedroom of the entire house.

In a flash, I am no longer standing in this meager home. I am now looking out over a concentration camp. Cold, stark concrete buildings litter a barren yard surrounded by angry barbed wire fences. A winter wind is causing snow to fall on this scene, adding misery and bitterness to this already bleak picture. But like little stars shining on the darkest night, children run into the yard playing. Even here, even in the midst of certain death, these children have found a way to choose life.

I stand stunned at the image before me, a numb stillness gripping my heart. Tenderly, Jesus breaks the silence. "Children can play in any situation. They can play in the midst of great pain. Now . . . " The scenery changes before us, and I am taken back to an image He showed me long ago. I am standing with Christ in a humble home, one that is overflowing with warmth and affection. I see God sitting in a wooden, Quaker-style chair as my big Jewish Papa, smiling warmly as He watches me, His little girl, playing with blocks on the floor of our humble house (see Chapter 1). I knew that this image was pure truth. I knew that this picture of the Father lovingly approving of His children's play was how I looked to the Father every time I chose childlike joy. Jesus puts His arm on my shoulder and says, "Children can play in any situation. They can play in the midst of great pain. Now, how much more so can my children play in the midst of perfect love, perfect peace, and perfect joy? Where my kingdom comes, perfection is released."

I look up into Jesus' gentle eyes. "Where you are is your kingdom, Lord."

Suddenly, I see again the vision of children in the concentration camp. But now I see the great big Jewish Papa-God walking into that concentration camp. There is an aura of tangible warmth and light surrounding Him; He is carrying the atmosphere of that warm cozy home all around Him into the camp. He carries all that the humble home is and represents with him, for He is that home. As the children see Him, they run into the glow that encompasses Him, closing their eyes in the solace that envelops them.

"Wow, Lord. You bring your kingdom. Papa's home! It's here. Even here."

Jesus stands there watching His Father hug and love on the children. "There is much to be said about a childlike heart. My kingdom can be amongst you, and only the eyes of a child will find shelter there [Matthew 18:3]. For of such is the kingdom of Heaven [Matthew 19:14]! They look and they find it because their eyes are bright and eager. No one knows the presence of their father better than a child. I could stand over a sleeping child's bed and they would awaken and smile because they know Daddy's home. Oh, there are many lessons here, child!"

The concentration camp vision vanishes and we are now back under the shaded canopy of our tree.

I inhale deeply, taking in all I have seen, knowing that what the Master has been teaching me is vital. "So, how do I keep this, Lord? How do I stay as a child?"

"LOOK WITH FAITH. AND KEEP A SONG IN YOUR HEART! CHILDREN LOVE TO SING BECAUSE IT IS A CONNECTION TO THE KINGDOM REALM."

"Look with eyes of faith!" Jesus replies with a carefree smile. "Always! Expectation marks the heart of a child. There is nothing more miserable and unnatural as a child whose hope is deferred [Proverbs 13:12]. Always see the best in everything."

"Like the children playing in Warsaw?"

"Yes, just like that. Look for joy and follow it. Look for peace and know that I am there in the midst of you. Keep your vision higher, simpler even, at times. But refuse to look with thought processes of arrogance, rationalism, and negativity. Look with faith. And keep a song in your heart! Children love to sing because it is a connection to the kingdom realm."

At these words I see a child across the garden playing with toys and singing a melody. Unknown to him, the song from his heart becomes a light-infused bridge. With every note of his simple tune, the bridge unfolds to the unseen kingdom of God illuminated all around like living light. He has no idea the reality that is enveloping him. It's a simple illustration, but oh! It is so very profound: his song has connected him to the Father's presence.

"Amazing! Simply amazing," I respond as I watch the simple song unfold.

"Yes." Jesus touches my heart. "Sing for me today, child. Sing and don't stop. Let the song be one of a childlike heart. Keep it before me in playful presence. If you lose your way, just sing again and you will find it [2 Samuel 6:21, 22; Matthew 21:15, 16]!"

Laughing, I say, "Awesome! I love you, Lord! Anything else? This has been fun, by the way. Oh, I hear the song 'Show Me

Your Glory' inside of me all of the sudden!"

"Remember, it is the pure in heart who see me, who see my face. The childlike heart will be a key to the greatest desire inside of you: to know me and to see my glory."

THE SOUND OF HEAVEN

One particular day, I was feeling weary in my ministry of worship leading and pastoring. I have always loved to sing but have never been extremely talented in either my quality of voice or the quality of my piano playing. I knew this about myself, and it usually didn't bother me too badly, for this one thing I knew: though it was small, I gave my talents to the Lord for Him to use—the foolish things confounding the wise!

But on certain days, I just felt like a failure. Every pastor has days and seasons and even years where they feel like failures. This feeling of inadequacy can either depress us to the point of exhaustion or propel us to cry out for more of His presence. Thankfully, my journaling was teaching me to bring even my worst days to Him in order that I may receive more of His knowledge on my heart. On this weary day, I sat with my journal in hand and this cry for more in my spirit. I did not know that the Father, once again, was about to teach me about being childlike.

"Lord, you see my heart. You see how I want to grow in faith, in grace, in glory; how I deeply desire my senses to be trained to know you [Hebrews 5:14; Deuteronomy 29:4; Matthew 13:16]. I think, more than anything, I long for this, God. Oh, teach me, Spirit of God! I don't know how it's supposed to be, how it's supposed to come. Just come. Just teach me. Just show me, Lord."

As I wait for Him to speak, I close my eyes and rest in His presence. I come fully expecting to see some picture with the eyes of my heart. As I wait, however, no vision floods my heart, but I do hear His voice. By faith, I begin to write what I believe the Spirit is speaking to me:

"Your song is your anointing, child. It is that deep well inside of you. It is not just music. The song is the groan in prayer, the language of tears, the melody and the harmony of compassionate cries, of broken sounds of intercession. And yes, in songs lifted high."

Surprised laughter escapes my throat as I confess, "Lord, I have to laugh. I mean, how ironic that on *this* day . . . the day when I feel like such a failure in music, you come and say, 'You are anointed in music.' That's just like you!"

I feel the Spirit's joy as He says, "See, you *are* learning my nature, child! You are growing in grace and truth! You are growing in faith. You will increase in my glory. By knowing my nature, you are growing in your faith. This is a way to sense me moving within you. What am I doing? What am I like? Where would I be working? As you learn more about my nature, you will know what I look like. You will sense me moving because you are familiar with my character and emotion. Sometimes, flowing in the anointing is simply walking into darkness and letting your light shine because you know that is what your Father would do. Stay close to the door of Heaven, child. Yes, put your ear up close and listen. Tell me what you hear now."

All at once, at His words, a vision unfolds within my heart. I see myself, with my ear pressed on a big white door, a golden frame built around it. I hear children laughing and playing with angels on the other side.

At the sound of their play, I am overwhelmed by God's Spirit. I begin to weep under the heavy peace and joy that fills the room. The glory that washes over me as I listen to the activity of Heaven is indescribable. I confess, "I have no idea why I sense you so strong on this image or on the sound, Spirit!" Still, I sit there weeping with joy and wonder, meditating on the sweetness hitting my ears. With tears rolling down my cheeks, I am suddenly standing on the other side of the door in the middle of the sprawling garden. I look across the rolling hills and see children and angels running together playing tag. Some are skipping and singing songs together. Another group of angels is sitting on the ground under trees with the children, teaching them games with yarn in their hands, games like Cats in the Cradle. Everywhere I look, angels are playing games with children, instructing them in fun. It looks just like a schoolyard recess: kids running and enjoying every moment of freedom given to them.

With mouth agape in wonder, I say, "This is the kingdom of Heaven!" Looking over the scene again, I ask, "What are you saying to me through this, Lord?"

At this question, I see Jesus walk on the scene. Up to this point, I had only heard His voice. Now He stands with me in the midst of the garden turned playground.

"Do you see all this, child?" He asks, hands motioning to all the exuberant play happening around us.

"Yes, Lord," I reply, weeping and laughing at the same time. "There is a weight of glory in what I see. What is the purpose of the glory here?"

Jesus takes me by the hand and we begin to walk among the children. "See all the good, child. This is the sound of Heaven. This is the way of the kingdom. This is what you are praying for when you ask me to let my kingdom come and let my will be done on earth as it is here [Matthew 6:10]. Fun! Joy! Joy in the Holy Spirit! This is the kingdom of God [Romans 14:17]. Righteousness, peace, and joy do not always look like what you expect them to look like! They are wrapped up in the childlike heart, child—for of such is the kingdom [Matthew 19:14]. These little ones see the face of their angels. They are not separated, for both long to be in the presence of joy. Living joy! They understand that their good pleasure comes from the Father. That they are made for pleasure and love [Revelation 4:11]. Child, this is the battle."

At this last phrase, I instinctively know that the Lord is telling me that the battle we believers fight is to remember that we are made for God's pleasure and love—to give love to Him and receive love from Him. That, no matter the responsibility of "working" in His kingdom, it is for the joy set before us [Hebrews 12:2] that we endure. I immediately think how hard this fight is for me, that's it not simply a battle to be won but an entire war fought over the course of my new life in Christ.

Jesus interrupts my thoughts and says, "Your mind is thinking that it is also a war, but your warfare must flow from here—from this place of childlikeness. What did I say about the kingdom? This is how you must enter. To these it belongs."

We kneel in the grass and a three- or four-year-old dark-haired girl with big brown eyes runs over to us, fingers halfway in her mouth. She runs right up to Jesus' side and He wraps an arm around her and squeezes her tight. She smiles and giggles with her wet fingers still resting in her mouth. Jesus looks at me, arms still around the child.

"Ask her what she sees," Jesus gently instructs me.

I am taken back by His command. This is the first time I have ever been presented with the idea of speaking to anyone besides Christ when I journal. I say a quick prayer: I ask the Holy Spirit to guide me and guard me from error. If the Lord is really instructing me to learn in a different way, I want to not be afraid. I want to simply trust Him to lead me. "OK," I respond. Looking into those adorable brown eyes, I ask the little one, "What do you see?"

Taking her damp fingers out of her mouth, but still keeping them close by her chin, the little girl says, "I see Heaven opened and the Son of Man standing at the right hand of God [Acts 7:55, 56]. He is here with me." She puts her arms around Jesus and hugs Him. I'm in awe. Her words are what Stephen uttered right before his martyrdom in Acts 7—a phrase I would never expect a child to utter or even grasp.

In astonishment, I sincerely ask the child, "How do you see this? Teach me."

Smiling, Jesus gently pushes the little girl close to me. She reaches out to me with a wisdom beyond her years. She places her wet, chubby hands on my cheeks.

She says, "You must learn to see as a child, with eyes of faith. You must see the impossibilities. You must see beyond what you are naturally able. If you can imagine it's there, it most likely is. The reality that you see cannot be seen without . . . it must be seen within [Luke 17:21; 1 John 2:27]."

I am struck speechless, dumbfounded at the wisdom this child has spoken. And yet I am also a bit confused; I am trying to connect all the dots from our conversation. Finding my voice, I turn to the Master. "Jesus. Oh, Savior. Make it all make sense. I want to see Heaven opened. How?"

"Look with eyes of faith, child. See what she sees!" Jesus puts His hands up in an "it's easy!" kind of pose.

Still confused, I cry, "But I cannot apart from you! I must see with your vision."

The little brown-eyed girl tenderly puts her hands over my eyes, blocking my vision. Then Jesus says, "You will see, for you are called to see. Open your eyes." The little girl removes her hands from my face. I am looking out at a massive tree in the garden. Kids are climbing in its branches and up its trunk, hanging from limbs, racing around the base. The Lord continues. "You see a tree, but a child sees a plaything—a castle to climb." As the Lord describes what the children see, it's as if my heart is seeing it too, as if my imagination is looking at it just as a child would. Children are climbing, not on branches, but on ramparts and turrets.

The Lord quietly speaks. "They see what is hidden—the reality that is hidden."

"Reality . . . " My voice trails off as I smile at the thought.

"It is calling things that are not as though they . . . " He pauses and waits for me to finish His sentence.

"As though they are reality [Romans 4:17]!" I exclaim. It's as if this Scripture has come alive in my heart for the first time. I am growing confident and excited to learn more. In great expectation I ask, "What else?"

Jesus continues by drawing His eyes and hands upward. "A child sees the clouds as creatures, as images, as things that are alive with life, shape, and form! They see adventure in the sky waiting to be discovered."

I look up at the vibrant blue sky and memories of watching clouds roll by as a child flood my mind's eye. Pondering His words, I ask, "How does this tune into the anointing?"

"Reality that is hidden is the truer reality. You must look deep, child. See what cannot be seen without, and see within to sense the anointing. Yes, close your eyes and breathe. Wait on me to show you images."

"And if I do not see?"

"Then wait," Jesus instructs. "I promise to teach you all things. The anointing *will* teach you. Wait upon it [1 John 2:20, 27]."

"Then see without," the brown-eyed child adds. She waves her hand and gestures toward all the children playing in the garden.

I smile. The image of them playing is beautiful. In a flash, I see the vision of me leaning my ear on the door of Heaven again.

Jesus says, "Yes, child. Listen for joy. Listen for song. This is part of sensing the anointing."

I look up at Jesus; He is standing beside me now. My heart is touched by all the Lord has shown me, but my mind is doubting how it is possible to tap into this when ministering in a dry service. The church I served in kept a strict time clock and strict tradition. Sighing, I ask, "In a church service, Lord, when I am ministering, how do I sense joy?" It truly feels like an impossible task.

Jesus answers gently, placing His hand on my shoulder, "Wait on me until I come. In my presence there is *fullness* of joy! Wait until you sense it. My presence is joy, is it not?"

I shake my head and confess, "I don't feel like I have the freedom to wait on you in a church service."

Jesus nods and raises His brows. "It is true that you are in a time crunch. Learn how to sense joy, then, in your secret place. You are smiling because you know how to sense joy quickly when you are with me."

It is true. I was smiling. "Yes! I laugh quickly and easily when I come to prayer!"

Jesus chuckles. "This is the anointing, child! This is my presence you sense! Do this in worship. Tune to this image you saw today, the garden where angels teach you."

Once again, at His words, I am in tears. Sometimes, out of nowhere, something He says just hits my heart! "I really think you are wanting angels to teach me things about your anointing. I am open to the invitation and say yes. I want to learn!"

Jesus puts His hand on my shoulder again and grins. "I know you want to, and you will. Lean in and listen."

BEING LED FROM CHILDLIKENESS

In all of my communing with God, it seems that the majority of the time He comes to me in tender goodness. And often in the midst of that goodness He appears in playful ways: a little joke here, a funny expression there, even at times doing tasks that I don't expect Him to do—tasks like putting a puzzle together as He lies on the floor. After spending time in the book of Ephesians one morning, I paused to pray about what I was reading, and this is exactly what I found Him doing. I entered into His presence by asking Him a question.

"Lord, what do you want to say to me concerning the workings of my inner man [Ephesians 3:16]?"

As I wait on the Lord's voice, I begin to see with the eyes of my heart. I notice Jesus sitting casually on the floor, working on an extremely large puzzle. Puzzle pieces are scattered every which way in seemingly endless directions. As I watch Jesus put the puzzle pieces together, I am flooded with thoughts birthed by the Spirit: the mystery of how pieces of Scripture, pieces of life, pieces of relationship, are being fit together by the Master's hand, the beauty of a piece fitting just right. I approach the Lord and see that I am once again a little girl.

Jesus looks up at me and smiles that glorious smile, then continues His work, saying, "The inner man is a mystery, no? A riddle to you until you see it all together. I am like the picture on the puzzle box. You see the picture on the box, you see the design, you know where you are going and how it is supposed to look, but each piece of your spirit—each moment of your life—is a piece that affects the big picture. Without one piece it is no longer formable. If you were to try to put this all together on your own, you'd be lost!"

I gaze at the enormous puzzle with its connected pieces and the still loosely scattered pieces all along the ground and shake my head at the overwhelming thought.

"Yes, Lord! It's way too big to accomplish!"

"You see, I knit you together in your mother's womb [Psalm 139:13]. Every strand of DNA, every minute molecule, I formed in you, child. And every mysterious part of your emotional makeup, the hidden part of you that is like a riddle, that which makes you you, undeniably—I formed and put together." Jesus holds up the puzzle box lid and says, "I fashioned you after the picture on the box, after the picture of the Designer: me!" I look at the box and see it is an image of Jesus. I smile. Jesus continues, "I fashioned you in my image [Genesis 1:27; Romans 8:29]. Every part of me is to be seen in you. One piece at a time."

Jesus holds up a puzzle piece close to eye level and studies it closely, turning it back and forth intentionally, slowly. Its edges are just a bit catawampus.

Jesus raises His brows at me and smiles. "When one of these pieces doesn't fit quite right, I can take it and smooth down the edges . . . " He gently rubs the piece with His thumb. " . . . and boom!" Jesus effortlessly places the piece into the puzzle. "There. It fits. It is my hand, the Master Designer alone, who can form what needs to be formed and fix what needs to be fixed. Yes, I can break what needs to be broken and mend what needs to be mended. I am your all in all. I make up the whole, and I am in the details. I am both to you, child—the whole and the details."

I smile as I ponder the Lord's work in my life, His work both big and small. "So," I say, "the things done to my spirit. Tell me more about them, Lord."

The image before my eyes changes and I see Jesus pushing me on a picturesque rope swing under our canopied tree. I am still a child. My white knee-length cotton dress moves with the gentle breeze, and I throw my head back laughing, swinging my feet to the rhythm of Jesus' gentle hand. I feel His pleasure in the atmosphere as I swing. I hear His soft laughter behind me. Although the Lord is barely pushing me, I am able to swing higher and higher with very little effort.

"Do you see how I push you? Not hard, but gently—and how the wind moves you with my movements?" the Lord asks. "One gentle push and you go up high. Yes, I got the ball rolling; I pulled you along and let you go and the motion was started. But I always stand behind you and push you into the rhythm with the wind. This is how it is in the working of your spirit: I nudge you, I give you a gentle push, and you are moved by the Spirit's winds, carried along to your next moment or destination, your next decision of purpose. The things done to you by my hand are always gentle and always in motion and they will never leave you stagnate. You will find rest in them, but you will never be stagnate. You will always be moving like rhythm and wind."

Jesus pauses and lets His words settle on my heart, all while still gently pushing me on the swing. Then He continues.

"How do you know if you are born of the Spirit? You are blown by the wind [John 3:8], moved by my Spirit. When you feel a tug at your heart, an emotion creeping up—yes, a trying, a testing, a refreshing moving there—then say yes to the nudge and let my Spirit take you up to the next level."

At the words "take you up," I am suddenly in a tree house looking down on my little swing. I am startled at my sudden placement and laugh out loud at the Lord's ways. Jesus stands on the ground looking up at me and laughing in kind. His eyes smile so tenderly as He looks at me in love.

"Child, you see yourself as a little girl here because you are made to know the movements of your heart. The actions, the things that I am doing inside of you and what I'm doing there in your heart—it's as joyful and innocent as these images."

I chew on the Lord's words to me. *Innocence. Joyful.* It sounds so wonderful, but I am left perplexed, for I know that often my walk with Christ requires effort and tenacity. I furrow my brow and ask, "But, Lord, what about the things that are done for, oh . . . say . . . warfare? Warring? For war?"

Jesus reaches His arms up to me and I plop into His embrace, making my way down from the tree. "Walk with me," He says, placing me down next to him and clasping my little hand. "You don't seem to understand my ways, child."

I am puzzled by His comment, but not offended in the least, for I have learned that anytime the Lord corrects me, it is always for my good and always accompanied by healing. With my hand still in His as we stroll along a seashore, I look up and ask Him, "How do you mean, Lord?"

Jesus picks me up and puts me on His hip and walks along the sandy shore, temperate waves dancing underneath His toes. "You see, I move in here." Jesus points to my heart, looks me in the eye, then adds, "And this is unseen. So, even if you are fighting a battle, even if you are in intercession, your heart can always be at rest. All things should flow from the place of innocence and 'for the joy set before you,' child [James 1:27; Hebrews 12:2]. So whether you are fighting the good fight of faith, warring on behalf of the lost or for your nation, always carry the weight of responsibility of childlike faith [Psalm 131; Matthew 18:3]."

"'Weight of responsibility of childlike faith'?" I ponder. "Did I hear you right on that? It sounds like a contradiction."

Jesus throws His head back and laughs. "To you it may seem strange. But child, there is no greater responsibility and honor given to those who see the face of God [Matthew 5:8], who sing in my temple and declare that I am God, the Son of David!" At His words, I see the image of children shouting, "Hosanna to the Son of David!" as described in Matthew 21:15.

"TO WALK HUMBLY, TO LOVE MERCY, TO DO JUSTLY. IT'S NOT DIFFICULT— THINGS A CHILD CAN DO. YOU ARE RESPONSIBLE TO GUARD YOUR HEART IN CHILDLIKE INNOCENCE."

Jesus continues. "You see, it *is* a responsibility. For to whom much is given, much is required [Luke 12:48]. But what do I require of you? To walk humbly, to love mercy, to do justly. It's not difficult—things a child can do. You are responsible to guard your heart in childlike innocence. *This* is responsibility on your part. Child, in these days of increasing darkness, do not let your heart be burdened with things that are too big for you. Always bring me the things that matter. I do not want you to stop seeking for justice and love. But, as you have learned, intercession is just as much about rest as it is war. In fact, the best warriors fight from rest, remember?"

"Yes, Lord."

Jesus smiles and lowers me off His hip and back onto the sandy shore, holding my hand once again. "So, walk with me," the Lord says. "Walk beside me, guard your innocence, and feel the nudging of your heart. Be led by joy. Be led by peace. Flow with me in the rhythms of my Spirit's winds."

At His words, I am drawn back to the image of that little swing in the breeze under our tree, its movements back and forth. "Flow in the rhythms of your Spirit winds. Like being pushed on a tree swing!" I respond, eyes brightening.

"Back and forth, to and fro . . . " Jesus says with a rhythmic tone and motion of His head. "A rhythm inside your heart: you speak, I speak, you speak, I speak—we listen, we breathe, we love. I nudge, you go. I lead, you follow."

Pondering this "spirit rhythm," I ask the Lord, "So, the things done to my Spirit by you are simply nudges that I follow?"

Jesus looks down at me and smiles, enjoying the process of my learning from His words and ways. Jesus starts a sentence: "Always hear my voice speaking, child, and . . . " As the great teacher He is, He waits for me to finish His thought.

Thinking for a moment, I look into His eyes and find my confidence. I answer: " . . . And follow. And whatever the nudging is calling me to do, always do it for joy and *from* innocence. Right?"

"Well said!" the Master responds.

And with that, the day's lesson ended.

This lesson of being childlike was one that could be summed up in two words: *trust* and *joy.* These two truths would appear over and over as I journaled with Jesus. These two gifts—trust and joy—are at the very heart of the King. As we approach Him in confidence, He gives us more joy and He gives us more trust. He lavishly pours it on us as He reveals His beauty!

When we see how beautiful His heart is, we cannot help but overflow in joy! Why? One reason is that as we look upon Him, we become like Him (2 Corinthians 3:18), and Scripture tells us that Jesus is anointed with the oil of joy more than anyone else in history (Psalm 45:7; Hebrews 1:9). He *is* joy! He is trust! So as we look at Him, we become like Him—a child of God who fully trusts his or her father and is overflowing with joy.

CHAPTER CONFIDENCE KEYS: HOW TO HEAR GOD'S VOICE

1. Believe that God desires to spend time with you just as you desire to spend time with Him. Approach Him knowing that He eagerly looks forward to spending quality time with you.

2. A childlike heart is vitally important to entering the kingdom of God, not just for salvation, but also for prayer time. Some ways to be childlike:
   a. Approach God in simplistic faith and with a joy that overflows with imagination and laughter.
   b. Play in God's presence! Spin! Laugh! Jump! Express your heart before Him.
   c. Sing, hum, or whistle as often as you can, not worrying

about the quality of your sound, but simply concentrating on the goodness of your Father. This will connect you to the childlike heart of joy inside of you.

    d. Ask the Holy Spirit for grace to carry this childlike joy no matter the circumstance. Practice sensing joy in your quiet time. Then, as you go throughout your day, return to that sense again in order to quickly connect your heart.

3. The more you learn about God's nature, the better you will be able to know what He is saying and what He is doing. Remember, sometimes what He is "saying" isn't verbal or visual at all—it's an impression, a memory, a song, or even being moved with compassion for someone in need. Know God's nature and you *will* know His voice.

4. Children see the hidden reality: they call things that are not as though they are, just like their Father does. Start to see the impossible in your world as possible.

CHAPTER CONFIDENCE KEYS: KNOWING WHO YOU ARE IN GOD

1. God sees you as His beautiful, beloved child. No matter what your earthly father was like, God is unmatched in His goodness as Father. He is the perfect Dad who loves to spend time with His kids. Let this awaken confidence in your heart as you approach Him.

2. The desire deep within you to know God fully and completely is *His* desire hidden in you. He longs to be in constant communion and communication with you. That desire in you, to know Him more, is a desire for His Presence, and He desires that you be with Him.

3. The Lord loves to hear you sing to Him. It really melts His heart. The Lord also loves to see you totally free in His presence, so

respond to Him as a child would, knowing that it's OK to just be you when you're with your Daddy.

4. Let your heart awaken to the truth that God is not religious or harsh. He enjoys spontaneity and creativity, which is why He wants you to know Him in childlikeness. It cannot be stressed enough: God really enjoys spending time with you because He genuinely loves you and likes you!

Chapter 4

LESSONS FROM THE BRIDEGROOM

Oh, the joy that comes in knowing that we are forever loved by Love! God invites each of us to simply believe that we are His favorite one, a child worth dying for, worth celebrating. When we allow this revelation of God's all-consuming love to teach us and mature us, we find another mystery awaits us: we are not only His children, we are also His bride. The love between husband and wife is a deep, precious love that cannot be compared to any other. It is a love born out of more than just kindred affections: it is born out of covenant and union: the two becoming one.

The word *know* in the New Testament is often *ginosko* (Greek), which means "to be involved in an intimate, growing relationship." It's the same Hebrew word, *yada*, that's used when the Bible says Adam knew his wife and she had a son. This isn't casual. This isn't just a friend to a friend, or even a father to a child; this is the most intimate relationship possible. It wasn't enough for our Creator to use the imagery of father and children to teach us of His love for us. He had to take the metaphor deeper. He chose to express His love in the form of a husband wooing his wife because He knew that married love is the closest form of love on earth that can compare to His matchless love for us. It's the two becoming one. He wants us filled to the brim with His very nature, and this only comes through union. The union the Lord has called us into is not a shallow one—it is a deep, mature marriage relationship. He desires us to be filled with Him: not just His word, not just knowledge about Him—but Him. His Spirit. His very nature possessing our hearts and minds.

The day a husband and wife say "I do" is a day of deep commitment, but it is also just the beginning of a journey that will grow sweeter as the years go by. Just as any marriage relationship grows and matures over time, so our relationship with Jesus grows. We have married ourselves to Christ through salvation—but that is just the beginning of a lifetime of deepening love.

This image of God being our bridegroom and we His bride is seen over and over in Scripture (Psalm 45; Isaiah 62:5; Matthew 9:15; John 3:29; Revelation 19:7). And this is often how He will speak to us in prayer: as the Bridegroom-God whose heart is ravished over us! Awakening to this reality, that we are loved as God's chosen bride, will chase away the shadows of doubt that Satan tries to cast over the garden of our heart. God really *likes* us. Yes, He genuinely cares about us. Our identity goes beyond simply being sons and daughters of God: we are His beloved bride, the one He has chosen to make an eternal covenant with. Oh, how deep His love for us! It goes way beyond God "putting up" with His creation—He actually *chooses* us. It goes way beyond God being our Father—He actually *woos* us. And

> AND IT GOES WAY BEYOND HIM BEING OUR BETROTHED—HE ACTUALLY *MARRIES* US. ALL OF CREATION COMES DOWN TO THIS ONE THING: THE MARRIAGE OF THE LAMB WITH HIS BRIDE.

it goes way beyond Him being our betrothed—He actually *marries* us. All of creation comes down to this one thing: the marriage of the Lamb with His bride. It's up to us before that day to learn all we can during our "engagement" here on earth. He's given us His heart and His word as a love letter to explore until that day when the wedding bells chime and all of Heaven sings, "Here comes His bride—all dressed in white."

Even so, Lord Jesus, our beloved Bridegroom—even so, Lord, come.

A TWO-SIDED COVENANT

As I entered my prayer time one morning, I was pleasantly bombarded with image after image of things the Spirit was showing me. I knew I had to still my heart and land on one thing, and I am so glad I did. For, on this particular day, I received one of the greatest revelations I have ever received. It all started with an image of me as His bride.

"God I am seeing so many images and hearing you speak. I stop and pause to tune my ear through journaling with you, Lord. Show me your glory. Come, Holy Spirit."

As I pause, I hear His voice: "I know your frame." Then I suddenly see myself dressed in a long, flowing white gown carrying a bouquet of flowers. I look just like a bride walking down an aisle approaching her groom. However, I am not approaching the front of a church or a minister's chambers: I am approaching the throne of God! An expansive throne shrouded in light and wispy, billowing clouds are before me, and the light that all this casts shines all around, literally chasing every shadow away. It is just a flash of the image, a glimpse of me in bridal procession. I knew that this vision wasn't just something God was showing—it was something He was *saying*. I cry, "The things that you are telling me are too great for words. But oh, I want to hear it clearly, Spirit!"

At this, the Spirit breaks in. "You are mine, child. *It is time for you to learn that I am yours* [Song of Songs 2:16]. Here in the depths of revelation comes a wellspring of knowledge and revelation about what I've called you to. The bride belongs to her husband as much as the groom belongs to his bride. It goes both ways, beloved. You are mine and I am yours [Song of Songs 6:3]."

At His words, I think: *Well then, I got the better deal!*

Knowing my thoughts, the Lord says, "You say you got the better deal? I love you more than you can fathom! You are my prized possession [Zechariah 2:8; James 1:18 (NLT)]! I left Heaven to find you! I claimed you with my blood! I would do it all again to find you! Your price is worth much: it is worth my very life, my blood, my all. You are not small. You have high value. What bride does not to her husband? What husband can look on the one his soul longs for and not be moved to pay any price [Song of Songs 8:7; 1 Corinthians 6:20]? So, you see, it is not just one way, it is two. I love you, and I get the prize. You love me, and you get the prize. It is how love is meant to be."

The same image as before floods my mind: my bridal processional to the throne. "Jesus, I keep seeing me with my bouquet of flowers coming down the aisle and to your throne."

Jesus answers to my heart: "This is where you belong." Suddenly, I see myself clothed in my bridal gown now standing next to Him at His throne. He too is clothed in glorious white garments and His face is adorned with the natural smile He so often wears. He gestures all around and says, "Yes, this throne room is your rightful territory. You have full access to my throne." He lifts His eyebrows and looks me square in the eye, smiling, with head tilted slightly. He points at me and says, "If you are mine" . . . and then He points to Himself and says, "I am yours."

Then He throws His arms out and looks about and slowly spins around. "Then this all belongs to you. You have access into the very presence of my love, without fear and without cost." He takes both of my hands in His and pulls me close, looking softly in my eyes. "You have the right by the cost I have paid. I am yours. What is mine is freely given you without question, child. You can come to my throne because I have freely given it to you . . . because I am yours." Jesus then playfully flings me out by one hand and twirls me around. Laughter spills out of me as I am released from His hand to dance and twirl in freedom. I spin and laugh and laugh and spin and slowly wind down to face my Lord, joy resting on my face. Smiling back at me in deep love, the Master continues. "You can come and dance in my presence in front of myriads of angels and sing the song that only you know—because I am yours. You have so much more freedom in me than you realize." I spin and dance and laugh again, heart overflowing with joy from this revelation. Jesus says, "You have barely begun to scratch the surface of all you've been given in me. I am yours."

I gradually stop and face Him, delight falling all around like a misty rain settling on my skin. He looks me in the eye with a zealous love, a moving seriousness. He takes my hands again and asks, "Do you see this revelation, child? That I am yours? This is huge! It is just as true as the other way around: that you are mine. *This* you understand. This you see because you were bought with a price."

I know that what He says is true. It is much easier for me to know that I belong to Him because He bought me with His blood. How could *He* be *mine*, though? I have paid no such price.

Peering into me with eyes that burn in passionate fire, Jesus says, "What price did you pay, you wonder? Love doesn't always work like that—having to pay a price both ways. Not in my kingdom. I paid the price and we both get the prize! I am just as much yours as you are mine. The angels do not have me. Creation does not have me. But my bride has me [Hebrews 1; Revelation 19:7-9]. You have me, my child. You have full rights and access to the things in my chamber."

An image of me casually opening one of the drawers in my husband's chest-of-drawers pops into my mind. Jesus says, "You have the right to pull from the drawers of Heaven and pull out exactly what you need [1 John 3:22, 5:14, 15]. Why? Because I am yours. *I Am. I Am* yours. You have me. Just as much as I have you. Do you see this? It is truth."

Once again, I see me gliding down the aisle to the throne of God, fragrant bouquet in hand. Jesus continues: "You come as the bride, unafraid, to the altar. You march up that aisle and you come knowing that I am yours. There has never been a truer reality than this, child. I have chained myself to you [Hebrews 8:8-12]. I am forever linked to you, to your likeness, to your position, to your humanity. I am giving it all to you. This is love. I do not merely 'put up with you' because you are mine. No. I am yours. You no more 'put up with me' than I do with you. Love is deeper than that. I do not look at you as the one I put up with. It goes both ways. You are my prize. I am yours [Isaiah 53:10-12; Philippians 3:12-14]."

His words have opened a fountain of tears in me. Tears—not born of grief, but tears of ravished emotions—flow. Weeping, I ask, more in sheer wonder than curiosity, "How is this, Lord? This holy, living God is mine? I must see it beyond legality. Show me, Spirit, more and more."

Jesus stands before me and gently lifts my chin so our eyes may meet. His eyes crinkle as He smiles and says, "My throne is yours, child. You pull down what you need by way of invitation, yes. But it springs from knowing that I am yours . . . not just that you are mine. Do you see this, child?"

Timidly, I respond, "I think so, Lord. Still, it needs to go deeper into my heart." It was just too much to take in at once.

The Savior says, "You have full access to the living God, the living throne of Heaven, because I have given myself fully to you [Hebrews 10:19-23]. This is marriage. I hold nothing back. No separate accounts. This is a joint account! We belong to each other just the same."

"It's hard to really get my mind around," I exclaim. "But, man . . . it's amazing!"

I feel His joy wash over me as Jesus says, "You have full rights and access. This is legal claim. But it is so much more than that. *You are loved. This is your claim. And you love. This is your claim* [1 John 2:5, 3:1-3, 4:19]. I am yours. Approach my throne like this, child. See yourself, not just asking for the legal terms from a God who loves you. See yourself as the one to whom God belongs. No man can own me. But no man can own you either. Even if you were a slave, no man really owns another. No man can own the God of the universe—for I made all things. I own all things [Romans 11:36]. Still, when you come to me, know that I am fully yours. We have mingled blood. We have mingled souls. We have mingled our beings together [Ephesians 5:25-32]. You ask of me and I give, not out of legal obligation, but because I see my wife, my bride. And I am moved by love. See this when you ask of me. When you fix your eyes on me, know that I am just as much yours as you are mine."

> "YOU ASK OF ME AND I GIVE, NOT OUT OF LEGAL OBLIGATION, BUT BECAUSE I SEE MY WIFE, MY BRIDE. AND I AM MOVED BY LOVE."

Exhausted by His love, I confess, "You'll have to open this up to me more. It's just too great to fathom. I love you, Lord. I am glad that you are mine. The God of Heaven, Master, Savior, ruler of all things . . . is mine. Belongs to me. Amazing."

THE WEDDING AT CANA

I believe it is of vital importance for God's people to understand the picture of the wedding that Scripture paints for us. We must understand what it is to be in covenant, what it is to be a bride, what it is to submit to His covering, and what it is to desire holy love even more than food. Knowing how deeply the Lord has intertwined Himself with His people is something we will never truly know until the day we see Him face to face. Isn't it amazing to think that all of history is summed up in the book of Revelation with a wedding? And to think, His first miracle took place at a wedding! If there is a truth the Lord is teaching us with how He started His ministry and how it all ends, I would say it is the truth of His all-consuming, everlasting love for His purified people. It is this desire to understand my position as a bride and all that Scripture teaches about God as the Bridegroom that led me to ask the Savior about His first miracle in Cana.

"Lord," I began one day in prayer, "I would like to speak to you about John 2:1-12—your first sign, the place you chose to manifest your glory. Jesus, it seems so trivial: no fanfare, no seemingly huge interest on your part to perform a sign, and yet I know you do nothing apart from your Father [John 5:19]. I know this story has absolute impact for my life. I also confess my weakness in hearing in these past many months. So, Lord, open my ears fresh this morning that I may hear and understand what you are saying to me today."

As I wait for the Lord to speak, I cannot get one thought out of my head: It all began at a wedding—and it's all going to end with a wedding [Revelation 19:6-9].

Breaking into my thoughts with an impression on my heart, the Lord says, "And, child, the journey for you is to learn how, every day, each and every day, to sup with me at the wedding table [Matthew 22:1, 2, 4]. Yes, it begins and ends with a wedding. But here and now, in this moment and the next, is a feast of hearts for you and I. Your journey is to learn to walk in wedded bliss until that Day [Ephesians 5:25-32]. And no, wedded bliss is not a simply hunky-dory, la-de-da, living-in-oblivion kind of love. No. For *married* love is *mature* love. It is deep love, it is sacrificial love, it is laying down your life for another, the two becoming one. This is the journey of marriage, child. You are learning how to live as a bride. Each of my children who will live for that Day are learning to live as a bride, not simply as my children—but as my companion, my co-heir [Revelation 19:7-9]."

His words weigh me down with glory as an awareness of Him settles in the room. I sink deep into my chair and meditate on this revelation. "Oh, Lord," I whisper to Him. "That's good. And so, so, soooo amazing. I know you've spoken of this many times with me, but I am still opening to it. Like a flower that I see now before my eyes."

Before me, I see a picture of a red rose opening up to a bright light and, somehow, in the mystery of prayer, I just know that this flower is responding to the light of revelation. I continue. "Lord, this light of revelation, this flower opening, is me opening to the revelation of your love, our relationship in the beloved. Amazing."

I do not see the Lord, but I hear Him speak. "So, look and see the picture, child, that John records in John 2:1-12. Remove all preconceived ideas and let me fill you."

"Come, Holy Spirit," I whisper as I wait for John's account to fill my eyes.

I wait on the Lord to show me His Word. Soon, I see just my sandal-clad feet and Jesus' sandal-clad feet walking side by side, as if I am a disciple walking beside Him on a dusty gravel road. I keep looking, and soon the image pans out to reveal Jesus and the other disciples making their way as a small group to the wedding to which they are invited. There is casual conversation and laughter among the group as it approaches the home where the feast will take place. As they walk closer, I can hear music playing in the courtyard just beyond the mud walls that make up the perimeter of the home.

The next image I see is of the disciples standing in the courtyard with Jesus, large smiles on their faces as they greet other neighbors with hugs, pats on the back, and customary kisses on the cheek. Jovial music fills the atmosphere mingling with the "mazel tovs" and "shaloms" of the crowd. I watch as Jesus joins the welcoming processional line slowly meandering toward the bride and groom, finally reaching them and kissing them both, in turn, on the cheek and hugging the bride tightly. The courtyard is filled with large tables, and many guests are seated on simple benches, ready to celebrate the feast, laughing and enjoying the fruits and nuts that the smiling servants lay before them in wooden bowls. The servants pour wine into simple pottery cups before each guest, keeping the crowd merry with every sip.

Beyond the table I see a large man with a salt and pepper beard, dancing to the music, his colorful robe swaying with each step. Somehow I know this is the father of the bride celebrating in joyous rapture. I laugh as I watch him dance, for he reminds me very much of the jolly Jewish Papa who God showed Himself to be while I was praying once before. I don't know if the Holy Spirit is revealing God in this story as well as the Son, but I laugh out loud watching this jovial father dance. The lively band forms a semicircle around him, keeping the man moving with each and every beat of a drum and strike of a string. I stare at the image for a good while, enjoying the atmosphere that I sense radiating from this merry man.

Eventually, I turn my attention away from the father and back to the Son. Jesus is smiling, His eyes crinkling in approval as He spans the crowd. Suddenly, His eyes widen as they land on His mother, Mary. Mouthing the word "Hey!" over the bustling crowd and boisterous music, Jesus walks over and greets His mom in the same way He did the others, with a warm hug and a kiss on the cheek. Then He gently touches her cheek and stares into her eyes with glowing affection. She reaches up and touches His hand, smiling back at Him. It is pure, sweet affection.

The sound of the disciples' voices calling for Him causes Jesus to pull His gaze away from His mother and turn toward them. Giving His mom one more squeeze and one more glorious smile, He heads over to His friends and takes His place next to them at a table. The master of the feast interrupts the conversation in the courtyard with a hardy clearing of his throat. Then, in a booming voice, He presents the young married couple to the crowd as husband and wife. Cheers, whistles, and enthusiastic applause erupt from the crowded courtyard. Jesus laughs out loud while clapping His hands. There is such joy on the Savior's face as He drinks in the image of the Jewish groom with his newly joined wife. He stares intently at the couple's hands intertwined, a deep understanding appearing in His eyes. Soon, His beautiful eyes spark again with laughter as the married couple is gaily startled by being halted into two chairs and then hosted high above the heads of the crowd—while still seated in those chairs—in a joyous exaltation. Clapping His hands again, Jesus chuckles out loud, but hidden inside there is a deeper joy, something unspoken.

I am aware that the look on His face speaks volumes that words could never express. I break into the beautiful scene and ask the Lord, "You understood this union, didn't you? I see you looking at them holding hands and I just know—you understood this with eyes unseen."

The Lord replies: "Yes. I saw the two hands intertwined as one. I saw each and every face celebrating this union and I knew: this is what I was made for. This is why I came: for *this* joy [Revelation 19:1-9]. When Mary came to me and told me they were out of wine [John 2:3, 4], I told her my time was not yet come because I knew it wasn't that simple. I knew I must die to bring about this union [John 12:23-33]. I knew the cost would be much greater than filling up jars and pouring out new wine. All of this would come . . . but it would not come without cost. So, there in the presence of such celebration, I was looking to *that* day when *the two would become one again* with my Father. She asked me to begin that day, but I knew the union would not begin for a while. I knew that the cost would be death, plain and simple, one laying down His life for the sake of another—for the sake of the mysterious union [Ephesians 5:31, 32].

"Still, she pressed on my heart to begin something I knew would never stop. And it hasn't, child. From the moment that first miracle began, my people have yet to stop pressing on the Father's heart; they have yet to stop pouring out the oil and the wine on a broken world, on wounded ones. They have yet to stop the miraculous flow of Heaven. Child, you cannot stop it. Maybe in your own life it can be stopped, but nothing will ever stop what I broke open that day for all the world to see."

"'For all the world to see?'" I question. "But it was just a small audience at the wedding."

"And yet the story goes around the world!" the Savior answers. "That's the power of one act of obedience."

"I see that!"

The Lord continues. "Child, many will look at the church in this world and say, 'They have run out of wine.' Even you, at times, have looked around at the condition of the church and thought, 'There is no movement of God's Spirit, no embracing of His heart.' But I tell you the truth, child: I am able to open the floodgates of Heaven and pour out such wine that you will not be able to store it, drink it, or give it away [Malachi 3:10; Acts 2:17]! All it takes is one small one, one tiny one, who is seemingly insignificant to the plan of the ages, to say, 'Father, we have no wine.' That's all it takes, child. And I am moved [Luke 11:13].

"See, Mary's focus was on no one else in that room. Learn from this, child. She came to *me*. Had she seen me do this before? No. But because she knew who I was, she drew on my heart alone. She did not go to the groom or the bride and burden them. She did not come to me worried or panicked

"SHE DID NOT GO TO THE GROOM OR THE BRIDE AND BURDEN THEM. SHE DID NOT COME TO ME WORRIED OR PANICKED AS A BEGGAR. SHE CAME TO ME AS ONE WHO HELD NEED IN HER HAND."

as a beggar. She came to me as one who held need in her hand, but with confidence of my ability to perform whatever she asked [1 John 5:14, 15]. In fact, child, she didn't even ask. She simply presented her need before me and never took her eyes off of me. Even when I seemingly did not answer her in the way she expected, she didn't take her eyes off of me, for she simply said to those who were serving, 'Do whatever He tells you to do [John 2:5].' She waited patiently in faith. She knew I would act. Why? Because she knew my heart and the power of God. She knew what I was born to do [Luke 1:30-33]. Somehow, she just knew, child.

"By faith, she saw the impossible. She had seen it before at my birth and that moment of faith was treasured in her heart [Luke 2:19]. Never doubting, always believing, she held onto the impossible nature of God. How she knew wine was important? That's a miracle of Heaven too, child. It may seem trivial to you, but it was a horrible faux pas in that day to run out of drink in a celebration. Mary was moved with compassion for the need. Learn, child. She was moved and put her eyes on me. When it seemed that 'no' was an answer, she poised herself, still, to receive [Luke 18:1-8]. Why? Because she knew my nature. She knew I would be moved with the things that move her heart, especially when faith is presented. So, she pressed in! Even when 'no' seemed to be the answer, she pressed in . . . because she knew my nature. How does this apply to your life, child?"

I pause and reflect on His question. Finally, I reply, "When I am asking you for something, Lord, even if it seems a bit trivial and the answer doesn't come like I expect, if I know your nature, I will still rest believing, poising my heart to wait on you to act. It's like I've heard someone say before, 'No answer is not an answer to prayer.' Guess Mary understood this, too!"

Jesus continues by simply impressing more truth on my heart. "Look at John 2:6 and 7. See how verse 6 is the number of man, child [Revelation 13:18]. Yes, it is true: I came to fill men up to the brim with living water, child. I came to pour into them rivers of living water that will not run dry [John 7:37, 38]. At my word, the water was poured out. Child, in your life as a pastor and a teacher, I partner with your heart, telling you to fill up my people with water. Fill them up to the brim. Just keep pouring in until it's full. This is what I did to my disciples. This is what I do with my people who will learn from me. I wash them clean, from the inside out, with rivers of living water [Ephesians 5:25, 26]. I pour into them life-giving water, child. It's not just my Word. It *is* my Word, but it's not *just* my Word. It is *truth*. See the difference. Yes, every word of mine is truth, but hear me: truth is not always received from the Word. But the Word is always truth."

Unsure of His words, I pray, "Help me hear, Lord."

"See, child." The Lord answers my heart. "Truth must be received in the heart because it is Spirit! My words are Spirit and truth, right [John 1:17, 6:63, 8:14]? But some will take only knowledge from my Word. They will turn it into something *they* do, not something I do in them. This pure revelation comes only as truth is received within them [John 8:32]. But even then, child, if truth isn't turned into Spirit—if it isn't coupled with Spirit—then there is no power to perform it in day-to-day life. My Word has power because it *is* Spirit [John 6:63]."

"If your word *is* Spirit and it *is* truth, why doesn't it automatically produce a good crop in us?" I wonder aloud.

Jesus says, "Because my word is *seed* [Mark 4:1-20]. Seed

must be received in good soil. Child, as you pour into your-self and as you pour into others the water of the Word, as you daily do this, it prepares your heart to receive truth. It prepares your heart to embrace the *Spirit of the Word* and the *truth of the Word*. The daily filling up with the Word is necessary for keeping the ground of your heart pliable and soft [Mark 4:20]. But even if one fills up with the Word and yet does not let it have its perfect work of maturity in the heart, then it just stays 'word'—knowledge. And knowledge *does* produce fruit, child. Do not be deceived. It does produce a harvest [Mark. 4:24; Luke 8:18]. But it is born of the soul and not the spirit. It doesn't mean that these ones are going to hell, but it does mean that the reward of abundant fruitfulness is not theirs, child."

"Wow." I ponder His words for a moment, then reply, "This is what Paul talked about in Galatians 3:21-31—the fruit of Mount Sinai versus the fruit of Mount Zion."

Jesus once again speaks to my heart. "Child, look and see again John 2. I told them, after the pots were filled, to draw some out [verse 8]. What is happening in the inner workings of your heart—all the time spent receiving truth as your own, taking it into your heart—prepares *you* to be drawn from [Proverbs 4:23, 16:22]. As you take in truth *as* truth and as you take in Spirit *from* the Spirit, then when you are drawn upon, child, what comes out *is* Spirit, not simply flesh [Luke 6:45]. It is a harvest of sorts. If you will allow my Word to fill you in the way it is meant to fill you—at the heart level, coupled with your inner man—then, without you even being aware, you will be filled with the Spirit. For my Word is Spirit *and* it is truth! You were always meant to be poured out, though, as a drink offering to a thirsty world [Philippians 2:17]. Which would the world desire more: water or wine? Both are needed, child. One sustains life, but one also makes the heart glad. I do not simply ask you to live on essentials, child. I invite you into the celebration, the feast of love [Song of Songs 2:4]! Wine may not seem necessary, child—but at a wedding? It most certainly is! And it all comes down to a wedding, doesn't it? So, which is more inviting to the world [Isaiah 55:1]? Not simply the necessary, but the delightful, the enjoyable, the grand, and the great. And this only comes by way of the Spirit. The world has received a lot of pouring out of water. And while this is good, the hour has come for men to be able to draw from your heart the wine of my Spirit. Child, without the Spirit on my words, truth is simply judgment. The Spirit turns it into love. Do you see?"

"Yes!" I exclaim as my mind finally catches up with the revelation flooding my heart. "It may be *truth* that some people's lifestyles and behaviors are not right with you. But the Spirit gives birth to love. Truths *must* be spoken from the Spirit in order for truth to come out loving and not condemning. We have given water and not wine. Wine goes down better [Song of Songs 8:9]."

"Yes. Rightly have you spoken."

"Amazing stuff," I respond.

Jesus resumes, "Do you see how this is manifesting my glory? Many had come before me and just given truth apart from the Spirit. But when I came with God's Spirit alive in me, I revealed, not only truth, but the love of His heart. This is what the world is hungry for. The truth will always be necessary, but the time to speak the truth by way of the Spirit is now."

Once again I stop and think about His words. In response, I say, "I also see, Lord, that we can be filled up to the brim with truth, but it is your Spirit in us that makes it possible to live the truth. I see it, Lord. Without the Spirit, the Word just fills us up with judgment, for by it we are condemned [Galatians 2:16-19, 3:10-13]. You took the Law and turned it into Spirit [John 1:17]! I love it!"

The Lord excitedly says, "Yes! Now you are getting it even more, child! *This* revelation here and now comes by way of the Spirit! I came to fill men up, not with rules and regula-

Under the Shade of Grace

tions, although I did give commands, but I also commanded my Spirit of *grace* to be upon them and within them, child. I gave them the ability to take all the Word and live it by the Spirit."

Overwhelmed by simple yet profound revelation, I finish our time together by confessing, "I love it. Thanks, Lord!"

A LOVE LETTER

One way a marriage deepens is by offering little acts of love and kindness to one another. A bouquet of flowers isn't just for dating relationships or holidays! The same can be said about love letters. You and I have been given the most eloquent love letter ever written: the Bible.

> WHAT STARTED OUT AS A ONE-SIDED LETTER OF DECLARATION TURNED OUT TO BE A TWO-SIDED DIALOGUE THAT BROUGHT GREAT REVELATION.

The Bible is filled with poetic declaration about how much God loves us. I decided one day to sit down for the sole purpose of writing a love letter in return to God. What started out as a one-sided letter of declaration turned out to be a two-sided dialogue that brought great revelation.

"Your face is sweet, my Beloved. Come nearer. Let me see those beautiful eyes [Song of Songs 2:14; Revelation 1:14]. Can you feel my love, Jesus? It is welling up, rising up like the ocean's tide; the very love you gave me is growing, and I give it as an offering back to you, my Lord [1 John 4:19]. You have put your love into my heart and it is real. It is good. It is pure and perfect, Jesus. I stand amazed at your beauty, at the purity of your love. Thank you for showing me truth for confirming the things you've been teaching me all this year [1 John 2:27]. I do not take lightly the precious jewels you share and freely give to me. I treasure them and vow to treasure them even as you would. Thank you for giving me, grace this morning to tune into your Spirit within so quickly. It's always amazing to me, Jesus, how I can find you so quickly! Oh, thank you that you never leave me but you're always right here, holding my hand. I feel your deep love this morning, and I thank you for it. I lay my heart down as an offering, as a gift to you today. Come, enlighten in my heart all that you want to say to me this morning."

As I soak in the atmosphere of love, I hear the Holy One whisper to my heart: "My dove, my fair one. You are sweet [Song of Songs 5:2]. Your love for me will stand the test of time. Yes! Your love! Why can't you believe that, daughter? Believe it now! Just as my love for you will last forever, you can believe that your love for me is not small; it will stand. It will last. This is all you want and, because you have let me form your heart and shape its contents, you will have what you desire. You want to know your love is real. Hear my confirmation today, child. It is. It is the realest love to me. Oh, it moves me beyond words."

I am weeping; I am overcome with emotion. To know that Jesus sees my love as real is too much to fathom. Love like waves crash over me as I ponder such beauty. Through salty tears, I cry, "Oh, you are so real, Jesus! It's like this love is living!"

"Truly, there is life in my love," Jesus says. "It is the very marrow of your being. It flows through you like a river, carrying strength, carrying nourishment, carrying defense against the attacks of the enemy. Just as all that the body needs is found in the marrow and blood, so is all that my body needs found in the living flow of my love for them [John 15:5]. This love was proved through my blood which now flows through you. My blood and my love cannot be separated [Romans 5:8; 1 John 3:16]. There are just some things in my kingdom that cannot be separated. There is an intertwining of truth, like vines that merge into one where you cannot see where one begins and one ends. This is the way of my kingdom. This is the way of my love, my cross, my blood. In receiving my blood, you receive my love. In receiving my love, you receive my blood. Truly, my blood is real drink [John 6:55]. It is a drink of love, the wedding wine of pure intoxication."

The imagery of His perfect blood given as the greatest token of love fills my mind. I whisper to Him, "Thank you, Jesus, for your blood." As I offer Him my thanksgiving, another image floods my mind: me, dressed as a beautiful bride. My white gown is almost blinding as the light of the cleansing blood of Christ has made me supernaturally pure. A lace veil rests over my head, shielding my face in a secret place to be discovered.

"Do you see yourself here, child?" Jesus speaks. "You are dressed in white, ready for that wedding day. Because you have taken the cup, you are waiting and ready for that day [Revelation 19:7, 8]. You are busy making preparations, final touches; but see how it's not burdensome. There is a joy in preparing for the wedding day [1 John 5:3]. Those who drink my love deeply understand this. Once you've tasted of the cup of my love, you are made ready for that day. I keep coming back to you in love, pouring it over you to remind you that I will wed you. I will not forget your love. I will not forget our agreement. See the lace upon your head. What I cover you with is a work of intricate, delicate beauty. My skilled hands have created the veil for your head. You are veiled with beauty and delight [Song of Songs 4:1]. What I fashion for my bride is perfect, and its beauty cannot be compared to earthly things. I have woven together a lasting covenant. Feel the lace between your fingers."

At His words, I see myself delicately grasp my wedding veil in my hand, tenderly moving the textured surface between my fingers. Jesus instructs: "Grab hold of that which covers you. Study the wedding veil of my people. See all that it means." I know at these words that Jesus—literally—wants me to study the Jewish wedding veil and Jewish wedding ceremony. He continues. "Understand: it is yours. I have covered your head. I am your covering. It is light. It is beauty. It is glory for your head. I am your glory. My love is your covering [1 Corinthians

11:10, 15; Ephesians 5:25-33]."

"Thank you, Jesus," I reply in humble adoration and secure love.

Jesus takes notice of my heart and says, "You feel that confidence? As you see yourself as the one whose head is veiled for her husband, as the one who is dressed and ready, there is a confidence that springs up! Oh, just stay here, sister! Let this image remain! My beautiful one! Seeing you like this makes my heart glad [Song of Songs 3:11]! I rejoice over you! Let me move with you!"

Smiling, I end my time with the Lord with an honest but simple, "Thank you, Jesus! I love you so, so much!"

After this special time with the Lord, I quickly followed His instructions and looked up the Jewish custom of the wedding veil. I was floored to have His words confirmed to me as I studied. The Jewish people actually have a veiling ceremony as part of their wedding celebration. There is a procession in which the groom comes before the bride and places a veil over her face. The Jewish people claim that this tradition started with Rebecca, the bride of Isaac, in Genesis 24:64-67. The veil is meant to symbolize an inner, hidden beauty, one that will not fade with time. It is meant to symbolize the bride's total devotion to her husband, the one alone who she has eyes for. It also symbolizes the heart of the groom, in that he will embrace all of who she is—the outward beauty, the inner beauty, and all the things he has not yet discovered in her personality and heart. This is him committing, therefore, to love her entirely.

> HE ALONE SEES THE INNER WORKINGS OF OUR HEART AND STILL HE CALLS US LOVELY. HE ALONE IS OUR SOLE DEVOTION. HE ALONE IS ALL WE SEEK.

Jesus, our Jewish Bridegroom, has veiled our hearts to be His alone. He has covenanted Himself with us in a lasting bond, promising to love and cherish all of who we are. He alone sees the inner workings of our heart and still He calls us lovely. He alone is our sole devotion. He alone is all we seek. And the mystery of this union is that God, the Holy One, seeks us, has pledged *Himself* to us. He embraces us, even in our weakness, fully and completely as His bride. We are veiled on our journey down the aisle, waiting for that Day when the two fully and completely become one. In the meantime, we are learning to love and to be loved as a bride pledged to the Holy Lamb of God.

CHAPTER CONFIDENCE KEYS: HOW TO HEAR GOD'S VOICE

1. An easy way to enter into communion with God is by simply saying, "I love you, Lord." Take a deep breath and close your eyes to free yourself from distraction and quietly whisper "I love you," repeating as necessary, until you sense God's love. Although you may not hear Him speak, He is speaking by drawing near. Just as a husband and wife don't have to use words to communicate affection, God often will simply draw near you and rest His peace, His love, or His joy on your heart and mind. Taking a moment to say "I love you" positions your heart to receive His love in return.

2. The Lord will often use "love language" in communicating with our hearts. He may remind you of His love by reminding you of the cost He paid on the cross. He may reveal His love to you through the words of a worship song or Scripture reading, or even through a pleasant memory stirred up in your mind as a gentle reminder of His goodness. God is love, so look for Him to communicate through love.

3. Take time to write the Lord a love letter. Even if you don't hear anything in return, write out the words that flow from your

heart. Just keep writing, telling the Lord how appreciative you are for His sacrifice, His love, and His blessings. This is a great tool to use to tune your heart to His love for you.

CHAPTER CONFIDENCE KEYS: KNOWING WHO YOU ARE IN GOD

1. The Lord sees you as His bride. He is in covenant with you: a covenant that He made and that He will keep. He has promised to love and to cherish you for "as long as you both shall live." This means it is an eternal love and an eternal promise! It is *His* promise to you, and you cannot break what He has promised for it was His promise to give!

2. Marriage is two people becoming one. It is two parties doing their part. Even as you have given yourself to God, He has given himself to you. Ask the Spirit to show you how committed He is to you, how He has fully given Himself to you as the lover of your soul. This revelation will awaken deeper love for Him and also awaken your understanding of how valued you are to Him.

3. The contract that Jesus made for you on Calvary was not just a legal, jurisdictional kind of process. It truly was a marriage contract. Because of that contract you have been made one flesh and have been given rights into your husband's chambers, taking whatever you need from Him because He has given Himself so fully to you. Remember, it is more than a legal right that gives you claim to Heaven: your claim is that you are His bride and that you are loved.

Chapter 5

LESSONS FROM SIMPLE WORDS AND PHRASES

What the Lord was doing in me through our time together was not only strengthening my confidence in hearing Him but also teaching me how much He really likes me. This may not seem like a revelation to some, but for me it was earth-shattering. For so long I had thought of God as "putting up with me"—loving me because He had to. After all, He is *God*. He *has* to love people. But journaling with Him was deepening my trust in how much He loved me, and this was truly freedom indeed! The idea that God really enjoyed me was setting me free!

As I stepped into this new kind of freedom, I found myself willing to take more risks in hearing. If God liked me, then I could jump out in faith believing He was speaking. If He *really* liked me, then even if I was wrong in what I *thought* was God, it was OK. It was worth the risk! This in itself is a vital lesson for all believers, especially those of us who were raised believing that God is, at worst, a harsh taskmaster who needs to be pleased, or, at best, a good Father but One is who is so holy He cannot leave room for us to make mistakes even if they are honest ones made in faith. My lessons with God were teaching me that when I am living for Him and by faith, it's OK to step out in new areas of belief even though I might not have a "clear direction" from the Spirit. For example, I wouldn't just shrug off an idea or a dream or even a word stuck in my head anymore, because maybe, just maybe, it was God talking to me.

Paying heed to those little words and phrases stuck in my head has been a fantastic teaching tool. As I commit my mind to God, declaring that I have the mind of Christ (1 Corinthians 2:16), I can trust that He will speak to me in my thoughts, even the ones that seem random or quirky. Does this mean that every random impulse is from God? Of course not! But even that is a lesson in itself! Learning to discern what is a self-thought or a God-thought is a lesson I am still learning, but as I learn more about His nature, the easier it becomes to know His voice from my own. And as I take more risks in believing that what I am seeing and hearing is from Him, the more I see He really is speaking.

What a thought: the God of the universe is communing with me. Add to that wonder how He comes to my level to speak with me most often, not in His grandness or omniscience . . . but, most often, He speaks through simple words and phrases running through my heart. He speaks to me at my level, and all I have to do is yield in faith at His Word. And as I do, I am suddenly no longer found "at my level," but I am brought up to His.

MERCIES

One morning I found myself pondering the word *mercies*. I knew this was probably something the Holy Spirit was talking to me about, so I decided to commune with Him through journaling. I had no idea that when I presented this tiny two-syllable word to the Lord, He would open up His heart to me in such a way that I was forever changed.

"Lord, I am captured by the word *mercies* today. It's come up a couple times in my day reading Scripture: 'Father of mercies' [2 Corinthians 1:3] . . . and I am 'crowned with tender mercies' [Psalm 103:4]. Just the thought makes me smile, God! Thank you. Thank you for mercies. I know there are depths to mercy that I have not even begun to see, let alone understand. Is there anything you can tell me about your mercies this morning? I wait for you."

As I sit with eyes closed, I feel the Father speaking to me. "I do adorn you, child, with mercies. I decorate my bride with my purest gold. I feed her on my finest wines and portions. I spare no expense for the one my soul delights in, the one my heart yearns for. Above it all is the crown of mercies and loving-kindness [Psalm 103:4]. Of course, you cannot separate my loving-kindness from my tender mercies. I am the Father of mercies [2 Corinthians 1:3]. From me, all mercy springs forth. Even shadows of mercy upon the earth were born in the chambers of my heart. Every time mankind shows mercy, it is a shadow of the great Mercy-Giver and His nature. Even the lost, at times, will show mercy. They know it is right to do, and when they do it they, too, reflect a glory that is found in me [Romans 2:14-16]. Do not be surprised by this. It is not only the redeemed who reflect me. Creation is not redeemed, but it reflects my glory. Man is my glory. The very form and nature of man is glory and reflects who I am [Genesis 1:26; Psalm 8:5]. But it is the redeemed who experience my glory firsthand, who walk in it and sit under its shade, who find it *ever present* in their being, fully glowing and shining like the stars or moon or sun [Ephesians 4:18, 19; Philippians 2:15]. There is a vast difference, but my mercies invite *all* to enter into it. And my mercies give the little reflections of me into the daily activities of even the lost. The little choices of mercy and love are

> "FROM ME, ALL MERCY SPRINGS FORTH. EVEN SHADOWS OF MERCY UPON THE EARTH WERE BORN IN THE CHAMBERS OF MY HEART."

reflections of who I am. It is my mercy that shines forth even through the lost when they show mercy to another."

His words stun me. I ponder how this could be true, but I am quickly reminded that *every* good gift comes down from the Father, that mercy is *his* fruit—not Satan's, not that of the flesh. Mercy is from God alone. "Wow," I reply, bewildered. "We could learn a lot from that. It even seems at times we could learn a lot from the lost when they choose mercy! I know this isn't the way it should be. They should be learning by our example."

I hear the Father impress upon my heart once more. "You must keep your eyes on my Son. There is a goldenness around Him. You are called to look at Him [Hebrews 12:1, 2]. He is the express image of my mercy. He is mercy spelled out upon the earth. In every language and tongue, mercy is spelled out in the name of Jesus. It shines. It glows. It summons all to come to the waters and drink deeply. It goes forth in power, for mercy is not weak. Mercy is the boldest, most glorious choice a man can make. It is taking the very nature of God, the very nature of my Son, upon them and choosing to walk in divine order [Luke 6:36]. It too causes my people to glow—that 'goldenness' that you are pondering."

"Yes, Papa." I am indeed pondering the sentence the Lord had spoken earlier: there is a goldenness around Jesus and how that glow is tied to His mercies. I cannot explain it, but there is *life* in the phrase. I ask the Father, "You said a goldenness is around Jesus. It makes me think of the bronze feet of Christ described in Revelation 1:15, like the glow from His feet is gold in color." An image of the feet of Jesus glowing like bronze fills my vision.

The Lord whispers in the midst of the vision: "Mercies. Mercies surround me." A living, soft, amber glow radiates off the vision of Christ's refined feet, filling the scene as the Lord speaks. "Mercies pour forth from my Son. My mouth speaks mercies. My tongue declares mercies. My song over you is mercy upon mercy [Psalm 145:9; Lamentations 3:22, 23]. The very essence of my kingdom is founded upon mercy. Think: long before mankind walked the earth, I was moving upon the waters and bringing forth life. This is mercy. You are wondering how this is mercy, child. I will show you."

Suddenly, I see myself riding on a white cloud, a cloud that I intuitively know is living and active. I realize: I am being carried by the wind of the Spirit. Together we fly over a beautiful landscape with rolling fields and verdant valleys, mountain ranges and abundant forests. I know I am looking down on a young earth, the earth just created as explained in Genesis 1. It is such a beautiful, diverse creation. From jagged mountains reaching up into the heavens to glittering waterfalls billowing down into crystal lakes, the Spirit is showing me all that the Godhead has created. There is such joy and love and even excitement in all I am beholding it's as if I could easily bust out laughing for sheer pleasure. Suddenly I understand what the Spirit is trying to teach me: this picture of a perfect created world was born out of and covered by the mercies of God.

I exclaim, "Oh! Your mercies are over all your creation [Psalm 145:9]!" I know what I am seeing, but still I can't put it into words. It is hard for mere words to describe supernatural revelation. "I see it, Lord! But, still, explain it better, please?"

With the vision of the Genesis 1 earth still before my eyes, I hear the Lord gladly explain to my heart: "Do not think of mercy as simply offering peace and forgiveness when it is undeserved. That is a glimmer of mercy, a glimpse at its beauty. Mercy is much more. Mercy is love. Mercy is giving life. Life birthed out of love is mercy [Mark 9:12, 13; John 8:1-11]."

Once again, I feel such life in His words: "life birthed out of love is mercy." Like a 3-D image popping off the silver screen, this sentence stands out among the others. I pause and let the weight of it rest on my heart.

THOUGH I WAS UNBORN AND UNCREATED, HE LOVED ME. THE MYSTERY IS SO HEAVY AND SO GREAT.

After a moment, the Lord continues. "Life birthed out of love, not just a desire to make things right when they are wrong, is mercy. But mercy is the very wellspring of my heart—to bring forth life to a dying creation or even to an *unborn* creation. It is love that brought you forth. In love you were created. In love you were conceived [Psalm 22:9, 10]."

In saying this, the Lord is not speaking of my natural conception as much as He is talking about His love and desire for there to be a *me*—an *Amber Desiree*—even as He had a desire in creating the world. He had a desire to create me. He desired *me* long before I was ever born. Though I was unborn and uncreated, He loved me. The mystery is so heavy and so great.

I hardly have time to ponder the beauty of it all before the Lord speaks again. "You see, I saw you in my heart. I dreamed of you in my heart long before you walked the earth. In my mercy, I knew you needed to come forth. You, my little dream, had to come forth [Jeremiah 29:11; Psalm 139:19]. So, what did I do? I gave birth to my dream. I said, 'Because I love the dream of my heart, I must give life to it.' It is my mercy that sees things that are not and causes them to come forth. It is mercy to see a need and then fill it with life. It is mercy to give a cup of cold water to one little one [Matthew 10:42]. It is mercy to give your time and your talents to those who are young around you. They may not have a great need that you see, but if your dream is to give them a chance to grow and learn, then when you give birth to that dream through your actions of love and time, you are showing mercy. Do you see, daughter, oh beautiful child?"

Tears are streaming down my cheeks as I respond, "Yes, God." I sit there silently basking in this great revelation, looking out on the world He has created. In light of all the beautiful creation that is before me, the majesty of mountains and grandeur of the stars, how can God say that I am His crowning creation, His dream? The love of God has entered the room and my only response is tears. Weeping, I say, "I am your dream. I am your dream."

"Oh, yes, my dear," the voice of the Lord whispers to me as He draws my gaze back to the beautiful creation around me. "I did all of this for you, not just for me. When I created the world I longed for it, yes. But I made it to be shared. I knew we would both desire it together. Mercy sees beyond self. Mercy sees the betterment of all around itself. Remember, do not just think of mercy as the righting of a wrong. It is so much more than that. Mercies are new every morning not because you are so weak that you need more forgiveness, but as the sun rises, so does my heart over this people, over this world."

I see an image of the rays of sunrise shining through my blinds in the morning, waking me up to life, to a new day. "You awaken and so does my morning song! I never stop singing over you or showing you mercy [Zephaniah 3:17]. However, when you wake up, we can spend time together, face to face! Yes! I am excited! You are awake! My mercies are brand new!" Joy is flowing off of His words like a flood as He continues. "They are as new as a sunrise. They are as new as a brand-new day. I am so excited to share my love and my life. I show mercy in that I am giving you love and life, new, every day. Satan wants to twist this truth into being a sense of me giving life 'mercifully,' as if I could snuff you out in a heartbeat and it's only my 'mercies' that keep you living. That is a warped perception, child. I do not think like that. I do not work like that. I give mercies abundantly because I give life abundantly [John 10:10]! See?"

Trying to take it all in is like trying to get a cup of water from a fire hydrant, but even in my smallest sip, I respond, "Oh yes, God! Help me rid this false idea of mercy! I want your idea alone!"

"Mercy triumphs. It roars a victory song," the Lord continues, speaking to my heart. "It is stronger than the grave. It is stronger than death. It is stronger than your sin [Ephesians 2:4; Colossians 2:11-15; Titus 3:4-7]. In this, I war over Satan, in that you are a brand-new creation through my never-ending mercies. But in this I also war: that I love you. My love is fierce. My love confuses the enemy. If he can warp your idea of my love, then he gets a foothold in my body. You, however, will not give him a foothold, child. You are standing in my love. By even asking me about mercy, you are learning more about my love."

I WATCH THE IMAGE CHANGE. WE ARE NOW STANDING TOGETHER IN THE MIDST OF EDEN, LUSH GRASS UNDER OUR FEET, EXPANSIVE TREES TO OUR LEFT AND TO OUR RIGHT.

I am astounded, almost to the point of speechlessness. Still, I manage to muster, "Yes, Father. I still see me moving over creation with you." I pause and watch the image of me riding the Spirit wind, looking over the works of His hands with joy. His manifested nearness is so close. I respond to the Father: "I sense your heart."

"What is it saying, child?"

I watch the image change. We are now standing together in the midst of Eden, lush grass under our feet, expansive trees to our left and to our right. It is a serene image, but the most beautiful thing to behold is the overwhelming joy across the Lord's face as He looks over all He has made. He is approvingly taking it all in, so pleased with what He sees. I drink in the image of my Master's satisfaction and quietly say, "Well, as we stand here looking over creation, I see that you are glad. I see you saying internally over your creation, 'This is so good.' There is a smile on your face, a living smile that pulsates from you. You are smiling over what you made."

"Yes, I am smiling because it was my dream and I brought it forth," He says. "And because I know that you will share it with me! Oh, for my dreams to be shared and enjoyed! It is mercy to bring forth your dreams. How selfish to sit on a good idea, to sit on the dream of your heart and never give it life. That is not love! That is not mercy. Dreams are put there to soar [Psalm 37:4]. Yes, child, even in you. Do not let fear crush your dream. Mercy, my mercy in you, casts out all fear. You are thinking, 'Wait, I thought that was love that casts out fear [1 John 4:18].' But remember, love and mercy are sisters, child: inseparable, connected together. You really cannot separate one from the other. Love without mercy isn't love. And mercy without love isn't mercy. They cannot exist without the other. It's like having a brain without having a heart. The two work together to bring life."

Laughing, I exclaim, "Wow. I like mercies!"

"And mercy likes you!" The Lord laughs. "Yes, daughter, I like you! I enjoy you! Why? Because I dreamed you into existence!"

"I like that, Papa!"

"You are mine, child. I called you by name and I like you [Isaiah 43:1]. I like everything about you. I see in you my Son. I created you to be filled with my glory, and I see it in you. I like your personality. I like what's being formed in you. I just like you!"

His words put a smile on my face. "Thanks, God! I think we forget that sometimes. Thank you for this love and acceptance."

He closes our time together saying, "Enjoy my mercies today. I love you forever, child. You are my forever love."

THE NAME OF YAH

Enjoying God's mercies while journaling began with a simple conversation prompted by a simple word: mercies. This single word opened my heart to an entire revelation on the nature of God! Whenever I chose to engage with a word that seems to be "just me," I find God waiting under a tree, a huge smile on His face, ready to commune with me. The lesson of learning to heed simple words and phrases is one of the most important lessons I have learned. Why? Because I find that this is how God most often speaks to me. God is not trite with His words, He is not careless with them. So if there is a word rolling around in my heart, it is a word packed with power that can be readily unpacked by simply presenting it to my Father.

Imagine, then, the revelation I found when I presented to God one of the smallest but most powerful words I know: *Yah*. His name. With great anticipation I came before the throne of grace, knowing that if He could blow my mind with the word *mercies*, what could He reveal about His very own name? All morning, His name had been rolling around my heart, so I approached God with His name on my lips, ready to position myself beneath our tree to learn.

> "Lord, you fascinate me. My heart is stirred by a noble theme [Psalm 45:1]! Your name! The goodness, the greatness of the Lord! I hear your song, Abba's song, over me this morning and my heart is swelling with praise. I love you, Lord. What do you want to share with me this morning? I want to listen and let you do all the talking!"

> I pause and wait for Him to speak. No vision floods my eyes, but a sense of His nearness lights upon me. I smile, and by faith I hear Him say, "My name is my goodness [Exodus 33:19]. *Yah*. It speaks life. It holds the world together [Psalm 148]. My name evokes praise among the nations. It is who I am. It is not just a description, for in it lays the very essence of who I am [Exodus 3:14]. My name is ringing over you this morning, child. It shouts over you that you are mine. Ownership rings over you: 'This is Papa's child . . . a child of Yah! The Most High God!' You are mine [Song of Songs 2:16; 1 John 3:1]! My name rings out over the mountains, over creation. It is sewn into the very fabric of my

creation, my DNA, seen in every living creature and corner of the world. My name is like the fingerprint hidden for the trained eye to see: on all the mountains, on every tree and flower, yes, in the very air you breathe—all around you. My name is whispered in the wind, hidden in the molecules surrounding you that fill up your lungs [John 1:3; Hebrews 1:3].

"I am found by those who seek me. I am found by those who look deep. I am found by those who will simply open their eyes beyond their worldview, even a little, who take the time to look 'beyond,' to lift their eyes to the hills. My name even brushes by the nonbeliever who will lift their eyes for a moment of separation from their worldview [Psalm 145:18; Acts 17:27, 28; Romans 2:14-16]. I am there. My name is there ever before them. Like a clue in a mystery novel, in the story written of my love all around them. Yes, I wait for my name to be revealed, and my name is revealed in you, daughter, in the sons of men who are the sons of God [Romans 8:19]! You carry the fragrance, the anointing of my name. But it is not just any name. Remember, it is my very presence [2 Corinthians 2:14, 15]. No other name evokes such presence. It is what it is for it is who I am. I am that I am. My name, my promises, are all tied into one. You cannot separate my name from my promise or my promise from my name. For I breathe in and I breathe out and it is done. I am not like you. I cannot breathe without hope being born. What I speak flows and is . . . and it is *only* good. It is good for you. Look into the mystery of my name, child. Look at it and see."

> "YOU CANNOT SEPARATE MY NAME FROM MY PROMISE OR MY PROMISE FROM MY NAME. FOR I BREATHE IN AND I BREATHE OUT AND IT IS DONE. I AM NOT LIKE YOU."

Once again I pause and breathe. I whisper His name out loud: "Yah."

"What comes to mind?" the Lord asks, knowing that at the mention of His name my mind is flooded with images and words.

I respond to my Maker with every thought His name brings. "Friend. Favor. Light. Power. Love. Compassion. Promises for today and tomorrow. *Yah.* Glory. Fame. The lifter of my head. Death to life. Life forever. Yah. Beauty. Awakening. Lord. Mercy. Truth . . . I could go on and on, Lord!"

The Lord answers, "These things are not descriptions. They *are* who I am [1 John 1:5, 4:16; Deuteronomy 4:24; Psalm 50:6, 73:26, 84:11]. I am the source of these things in you. They may describe you, your heart, your position, your moment in time, but as for me—they *are* me. It *is* who I am. My name is all of these things and more. My name unfolds like a ladder that goes on and on."

As He speaks these words, a picture appears in my mind's eye. I see way up in the heavens the unrolling of an enormous rope ladder. I stare up and down its length and find that it rolls on and on and on. I know this ladder is eternal. Somehow I just know that the spaces between its rungs are the size of an entire universe, and yet I am able to gauge the next step. The Lord breaks in as I ponder the scene: "Every rung in the ladder opens to a whole new plane of exploration and existence."

All at once I understand: each step on the ladder is an aspect of God's name! It is so large, so vast, one could never explore each step. I see myself step onto one rung of the ladder and it becomes a whole world that opens before me, looking just like the Garden of Eden in appearance, teeming with plants and life. What was simply a step on a ladder has somehow become an entire realm to discover. Each rung is the same: another level, another world, another truth of who He is! What, to us, is simply a name is actually an entire unending realm to discover.

Once again, I see this vast ladder before me. Shaking my head in wonder, I say, "Oh, Lord! How could we ever conquer even one level of who you are [Romans 11:33; 2 Corinthians 2:9, 10]? How can I ever be knowledgeable about you? Even a little? Oh, I want to know you! I don't want to miss anything! And yet . . . I know I'll never know it all."

I see Him take me by the hand. He stands before me dressed in His usual white, simple garments, wearing His favorite accessory: His glorious smile. "Daughter, allow me to show you what is needed for today. I desire to show you the most intimate parts of my being. I desire to show you that which will heal you, bind up your wounds, seal your heart in fiery love, and baptize you in depths of love and forgiveness [Psalm 147:3; Song of Songs 8:6; Ephesians 3:17-19]. Because you desire more than a drop, I have reserved for you the store-rooms of Heaven to explore."

"Oh, Lord!" I exclaim, overcome by His generous offer.

"Not everyone desires to know me more," He explains. "I know it's hard for you to fathom. Some take my name in vain. They do not seek it as a treasure, as a vast ocean to be explored."

Suddenly, I see a treasure map before my eyes, and somehow I know it is a map of His name. I study the map and see a red line that travels over the landscape that is *Yah*, leading to one incredible destination after destination, over mountains and hills, lakes and seas. Every truth of who He is reveals treasure. Following this map causes me to find treasure not only at my "X marks the spot" final destination of Heaven, but all along the way! Every single step leads to treasure! I cannot help but laugh as I look at it.

The Lord says, "My name reveals who I am, my nature, my character. My very DNA is revealed and discovered in my name. My name carries weight [Exodus 34:5-8]. It carries power. It carries the antidote needed for every situation you face. My name spoken into a situation is like a prescription to cure the disease. I am the Prince of Peace when you need peace [Isaiah 9:6]. I am the Lord of the Sabbath when you need rest [Matthew 12:8]. My name remains the same, although it is many-faceted. It is all one in the same, for I am all one in the same [Deuteronomy 6:4]. The God whose name is Judge is also the God whose name is Mercy. The God whose name is Almighty is also the God whose name is Servant [John 13:13, 14]. I am all in all. I am in all and in you, child. You are in me and I am in you. You carry my name. Every one of my names is in you. You have been given all things that you need right inside of you, and they can be released and accessed at just the mention of my name [2 Peter 1:2-4].

> "MY NAME IS FREELY GIVEN TO ALL WHO WILL RECEIVE IT. MY NAME RESTS; IT HOVERS OVER ALL OF MY CREATION. CREATOR. MIGHTY GOD. MERCIFUL FATHER."

"If you need healing, speak my name as Healer. If you need victory, speak my name as Jehovah-Nissi [Exodus 17:15]. I am all in all to you. Trust me in this. My name is power and life. My name is freely given to all who will receive it. My name rests; it hovers over all of my creation. Creator. Mighty God. Merciful Father. It is seen in the mountains, in the trees, in the delicate design of a newborn baby. My name is power and life. I am in my name and my name is in me. Every time you declare my name, child, you shift the atmosphere around you. When you declare my name you declare my greatness. You are speaking light out of your mouth. It is like a shaft of power and light, unseen to you but seen in the spiritual realm every time you declare my name. When you speak it, demons flee because they see the power released [Psalm 8:2, 68:1-4; Luke 10:17-20]. Remember, it is like a melody exuding from within you when you speak it—a sound that is heard and a sight that is seen in the spirit realm. Yes, demons hear it and see it and flee. My angels see it and stand at attention.

They are drawn to the sound and the melody of my name being poured out of my people. They stand, ready to serve the children of my name [Psalm 91:11-15].

"My name gives life to those who despair. It is like water poured forth on thirsty ground. When you speak my name over a dry, dead situation, it is life-giving. It causes springs to spring forth from the earth. When you speak my name over a dry heart, it is life [Numbers 6:27; John 11:25]. You may not see it, but such power is released, daughter. When my name is declared from your lips, you change the atmosphere. Believe it, child! When you sing my glories, my name over the congregation even as you did last night, things happen! When you declare Yahweh, Yahweh God over the people, and declare that my name is compassion, my name is graciousness . . . then grace and compassion are poured out excessively from above upon them [Exodus 34:6, 7].

"You may not see it but do not judge by what you see. Believe me, child, my name is released and doing things. It releases my very nature around you and through you. You can draw on my name at any time. My name is like a bank account, full of the deposits that you need. You can draw on me for grace, peace, power, provision, direction—it is all in my multiple names, which are all one in the same. Multiple accounts from one source. Whatever account you need, whatever currency you need, call on that name [Mark 16:16-18]. Peace. Love. Life. Righteousness. It is all yours, your inheritance, because now it is your name. I am in you. My name goes with you. It covers you. I am yours.

> "IT IS ALL YOURS, YOUR INHERITANCE, BECAUSE NOW IT IS YOUR NAME. I AM IN YOU. MY NAME GOES WITH YOU. IT COVERS YOU. I AM YOURS."

"Names matter much, child. The name carries the identity of the person. My name carries my identity, as does yours. If my name is in you, then my identity is in you. My life, my power, is in you. All the rights associated with that name are in you [John 17:11, 22-26]. Names carry weight. This is why I give you a new name [Revelation 2:17]. Your name carries your new identity. I call you by that name. Your spirit knows it. It is my name upon you. I love you, child. You are mine. You have my name. Now, believe that you have received it."

MIGHTY

A number of years ago I joined with many other believers in praying for a young man who was very ill. Countless prayers had been offered up for this boy with even well-known pastors and ministers agreeing with us in prayer throughout the nation. We were unafraid to ask God to heal this young man for it was clear to each of us that it was God's will to heal. Jesus healed all who came to Him. The Lord declared Himself to be Jehovah Rophe, our healer. We knew this with unwavering certainty.

So when the young man passed away after many months of much suffering, my heart was heavy. Tears flowed. Disappointment taunted my mind. But because of the faithfulness of God in past seasons, I knew He was still good and that, even now, I could bring this pain to Him. I didn't intend to bring it to Him on the particular day I ended up doing so. It started out by my heart declaring an aspect of God's nature over and over again: mighty. He is mighty. Elohim, the God of all might. With the witness of His Spirit resting on that word—mighty—I knew it was an open invitation for conversation. So I sat down to write.

"Lord, once again this morning, I am drawn to your name: Elohim. But what is striking a chord in my heart today is mighty: that you are Mighty Creator. Mighty God. Mighty in power. Somehow today, Lord, I need to know you are mighty. I in myself am far from mighty. But, oh God, you are: You are mighty. Speak to me this morning about your might."

I pause and wait on the Mighty One to speak, the word *mighty* bobbing around on the still waters of my heart like a fishing lure waiting for a bite. Only, in this scenario, I am the one who is caught and pulled deeper into the waters of my heart, where revelation washes over me. So I pause and wait with the word—"mighty, mighty, mighty"—calling to God in prayer.

Then the Spirit speaks.

"Child, I know you are trying to find words to describe my might, but words will fail you [Job 38–39]."

He pauses a moment and lets me chew on what He has spoken. Then He continues.

"You have no grid within yourself to find and define might. But if you look at me, you will find that grid. Although finite in your believing, you still have the ability—the eternal ability to know and understand the God of all power, of all sufficient might [1 Corinthians 2:16]."

He pauses again. I smile in wonder.

Then He continues again. "See for yourself, child."

All at once I am staring into the black canvas of space delicately lit up by countless twinkling lights.

"Child," the Lord says, "you do not simply love stars for their beauty or vastness. It is the fact that they are impossible to be created apart from an eternal God—apart from a good, all-knowing, ever-loving God. I put these stars into the heavens and I call them each by name [Psalm 147:4]. Not one falls from the sky that I do not see and sense. They came from me; they came from my imagination. They came from my mind. This is what my mind creates, child. Stars, mathematics, physics: I formed it all within my being."

I laugh out loud at the thought of what God creates versus what I create! Chuckling, I say, "And here I am pleased to crochet something or make a little doily!"

I feel the Lord smile as He prompts. "Oh, child, you are filled with creative power too. But your best mathematician, your greatest scientist, your most fantastic artist, brain surgeon, or philosopher will never come close to my matchless ways [Exodus 15:11; Isaiah 40:6-8]."

"So true," I agree.

Unexpectedly, I see an image of myself crying at the thought of this might! I am sitting under the shade of my tree and Jesus is seated next to me. I bury my head in Jesus' shirt, sobbing. A question is running through my mind—in fact, it is *the* question. But I'm afraid to ask it.

"Go ahead, love," Jesus says as He wipes my hair away from my eyes, encouraging me to ask even the hardest thing of Him.

Embraced by His tender hold, I fiddle with His shirt momentarily before I find the strength to ask, "Lord, I know you are mighty and hold all power. So, why did the little boy have to die?"

Jesus holds me in silence for a moment as the heavy question hangs in the air. Then, quietly, He speaks.

"Sometimes, child, there are no answers on this side of this tree [1 Corinthians 13:9-12]. When you cross over, you will find all peace, all knowing, and then will see as I do. But for now, you must see with eyes of faith. Faith requires you to not always see—but to simply believe [John 20:29; 1 Peter 1:8]."

His answer brought me pause. It was so simple. "Wow. I've never really thought of it so clearly," I confess.

With all the tenderness of a gently instructing father, Jesus continues. "You, in your humanness, want a list of why things don't work out. You want a checklist to say, 'This is where we missed it.' You are always trying to figure out why healing doesn't come, why it doesn't work, what you can do differently. Child, I'm telling you that you are simply called to *believe* [John 6:29]. And when the answers do not come, you are still called to simply *believe*. I know that when a death occurs that seems out of my plan, the questions will naturally rise. I don't mind the questions, child, as long as you come back to the right answer."

Casting my eyes to Him, I ask, "And the answer is?"

Smiling eyes stare back at mine and answer, "To believe." Jesus keeps His gaze resting on me and pauses with tender mercies visible on His beautiful face. With a slight nod of His head, He softly says, "That's all that is required of you here and now. To believe that I *am* Almighty God, who split open the heavens, holds the earth within His hands, and who holds time and circumstances there too [Psalm 31:15]."

A nagging thought invades my mind as I ponder His words. This time unafraid, I inquire, "But God, you see this need to walk balanced between sovereignty and responsibility. Can you sort it all out?"

Jesus genuinely laughs at my question, and I know at once: He is laughing, not at me, but at the purity of my question. He is actually delighted in it. "Of course I can," Jesus responds with merriment lacing His words. "But I *do* give you the tension, it's true, in order that you have to fully rely on me."

"That makes so much sense." The simplicity of His answer is so amazing.

Jesus continues. "It is here in the tension of your responsibility and my sovereignty that you wrestle with truth, leaning one way and then leaning another. Child, this is how it's meant to be until the day your faith is made sight [2 Corinthians 5:7]. You are called to keep doing what you know to do: not making excuses like some do for why they *don't* contend in prayer, but also not looking for a list or require-ments and answers or formulas to follow. You are simply called to believe like a child and to just keep believing when you don't see it come [Matthew 18:2-4; Hebrews 11:1]."

At His words I begin to think about all the books I have seen on healing, deliverance, and the like. So many books with so many formulas. It was just a thought lighting upon my mind, not one spoken on my tongue, and yet even this Jesus addresses. "No," He says, "I do not condemn those who write books on healing. Many of them are well needed, child. Some, however, do turn faith into formula, and this I do not like." He says this with brows raised.

After another brief pause from pondering all of His wisdom, I answer, "Lord, I really see that my obedience is about doing just that—believing and not necessarily seeing the answers come."

"Child," He speaks affectionately. "If you make your obedience about seeing the answers come then you *do* make it about *results*. You *do* turn it into a checklist. However, if you sim-ply fix your eyes on me and make your obedience all about follow-ing me, about believing who I am, then no matter what happens, your belief will not change [Hebrews 6:19; 1 Peter 1:8]. Your eyes will still be fixed on the author and the per-fecter of your faith [Hebrews 12:2]. *You are not called to results, but to belief.* You are not called to per-fection in what you do, either. You are called to holiness, yes. But how does it come except through faith!"

> "I HAVE ALL THE ANSWERS FOR TOMORROW. YOU WILL HAVE THEM ALL IN THAT DAY. FOR NOW, JUST KEEP BELIEVING."

"So true," I confess as I muse over all He has spoken. "This helps me, too, this morning to rest in *your* might and not in my own."

Jesus ends our time together by stating the simple truth. "I have all the answers for tomorrow. You will have them all in that day. For now, just keep believing."

God our Father so loves to reveal His name, His nature, and His ways to us that He is willing and ready to unpack out of one small word depths of truth that we could never fully fathom. We must come boldly to the Father believing that if we are hungry to learn from Him, He is eager to teach us. We should never fear raising our hand to ask a question from our Great Teacher. No question is too small, too stupid, or too "out there" for Him. Learning to recognize little words and phrases as an invitation to learn from the Master will transform what we write off as "nothingness" into greatness.

CHAPTER CONFIDENCE KEYS: HOW TO HEAR GOD'S VOICE

1. Take a risk. It takes faith to hear from God (Hebrews 11:6), and faith is often a risky thing (Hebrews 11:7-39). A safe place to start taking little risks is by bringing random thoughts to God as a point of conversation. Ask the Holy Spirit to help you take note of these "random" words and phrases. Then simply present them to God, asking Him what He wants to teach you through them. He is ready to teach you!

2. Look to Jesus. This cannot be stressed enough. By continually setting the eyes of your heart to see Him, you are coming to the mediator who gives you access to the kingdom of God. Set the eyes of your heart on Jesus by meditating on Scriptures about Him, by reflecting on the cross and what He has freed you from, by simply picturing Him on the cross or on His throne. Simply put: just keep it all about Jesus! By continually aligning yourself to glorify Jesus alone, you will have ears to hear and eyes to see.

CHAPTER CONFIDENCE KEYS: KNOWING WHO YOU ARE IN GOD

1. God really likes you. Let this truth wash over you. He doesn't think you are stupid. He doesn't think you are "uncool." He really, really likes you and thinks about you all the time.

2. Think about what Jesus has done for you. His mercies are poured out on you new and fresh every day! He did not shed His blood for you out of duty. He shed his blood for you because of His great love. Remind yourself that you did nothing to earn His forgiveness or love—He made the way when you couldn't. Why? Because He greatly desires that you be with Him where He is. Let this truth bolster your confidence and awaken your praise!

3. You are the dream of God's heart. He desires for you, His dream, to enjoy His blessings. He loves to see you come alive in the things He designed you to be passionate about. He created you for partnership, for communion, and placed you in this world to enjoy all it holds. Dare to enjoy everyday life with your Creator!

4. God has given you His name. Even as a husband gives a wife his last name, you are given God's holy name. Everything His name is and represents is now yours through Christ. This is why He calls you holy: for His name is Holy Spirit, Holy Father. Don't you see? You are not small! You matter so much to God that He gave you the *right* to bear His name and carry His authority! Awaken to the name you've been given.

Chapter 6

LESSONS FROM THE SONG GIVER

One of the ways the Spirit has taught me to recognize His voice is by tuning, not only to the words and phrases in my head, but also to the song that is on my heart. I often wake in the morning with a song running through my head. For years I thought I awoke like this because I love music. However, as the Spirit taught me about the nature of His voice, I found myself heeding the lyrics that were swirling in my mind when I awoke each morning. Waking with a song shows me that somewhere in the night my spirit was singing to God (Song of Songs 5:2)! Even better: *He* was singing to me (Zephaniah 3:17; Psalm 32:7)!

If I sit down to pray and a song is suddenly ringing within me, I know God is most likely highlighting that song as a point of worship, focus, or conversation between us. For instance, if I sit down to pray, quieting myself before Him, and the words to "How Great Thou Art" come to mind, I know that those lyrics are a great jumping-off point to first worship Him and then allow the song lyrics to highlight things about Him for us to talk about. Sometimes, the words of a song are things God is speaking to me about how He sees *me*! A funny example of this: One day I heard the old song by the band The Turtles, "So Happy Together," on the radio. The next day, I heard it again. Later that day, I was scrolling through the *TV Guide* when I saw the title of a movie pop up—not once but twice. The title of the movie? "So Happy Together." I finally stopped and said, "Lord, maybe this is coincidence, but it just might be you talking. So, what are you saying through this song?" I paused to listen and heard Him whisper the lyrics of the song to my heart: "I can't see me loving nobody but you for all my life!" I laughed out loud as the beauty of being God's favorite (which we *all* are) washed over me. Oh, how He loves us so! He simply wanted to let me know in a creative, musical way. So I sang the song out loud back to Him and laughed myself silly with the joy of the song on my heart, receiving the revelation of love the Lord was singing over me.

> HE SIMPLY WANTED TO LET ME KNOW IN A CREATIVE, MUSICAL WAY. SO I SANG THE SONG OUT LOUD BACK TO HIM AND LAUGHED MYSELF SILLY WITH THE JOY OF THE SONG ON MY HEART.

Yes, singing is a quick way to tune one's heart to the Father for multiple reasons. For one, it takes your mind off of yourself and puts it on Him in a fun, artistic fashion. We can find ourselves engrossed in the study of His Word and in commentaries and listening to sermons—and all of this is awesome. But when we throw off the seriousness of study and just sing? Ah, wonderful lightness comes to our hearts! It taps into the unhindered expression that man was made for: creativity. God delights in creativity. He adores it in His children, and music is the easiest way to tap into that aspect of who He made us to be. And whenever we tap into who we were originally designed to be? That brings us to an entirely different place with God.

And this thought leads us to another reason singing is great for connecting to God. It is found in the lessons I have already shared: singing is a very childlike thing to do. I had the great privilege of teaching music to children, and I can say this with certainty: every child loves to sing! They have no inhibitions about their voice or their body movements. They just go for it with all they have, especially if the song is fun and silly.

Singing is also a great way to tap into the childlike quality that God taught me is necessary to easily hear Him: joy. Joy easily bubbles up when we sing praises to God. It is part of losing our serious adult nature and letting ourselves just have fun with Daddy-God! So, as you step out in journaling, an easy place to start is through a song of worship to the Lord. Sing to Him. Hear Him singing to you. And then ask the Spirit exactly what He is communicating. You will be surprised at all the Lord unpacks as we sing a song of love.

ODE TO JOY

Any song that makes you smile is a great one to talk to God about, especially when journaling. One such song on my heart one morning was fully appropriate, then, to sing to the Father and to connect my heart with Him in journaling.

I begin my time with the Lord by quieting myself, eyes closed. Immediately, I hear in my heart the beautiful song, "Ode to Joy." I swirl the lyrics to the ancient hymn around my heart, closing my eyes as I meditate on their truth.

Joyful, joyful we adore Thee, God of mercy, Lord of love
Hearts unfold like flowers before Thee, opening to the sky
above[4]

As the sweet melody echoes in my soul, I suddenly hear Jesus say, "The life of the Spirit is one of joy [Romans 14:17]. Yes, I have been speaking to you much about this. Joy is a key component of my heart. It cannot be separated from my being and therefore cannot be separated from the one who is in me. In me you live and move and have your being [Acts 17:28]. I am in you and you are in me. My nature has taken over yours. It is there—and joy is a key factor in expressing who I am in you."

"That's why you smile a lot!" I respond in kind—and with a bright smile on my face.

"I have much to be happy about!" I hear Jesus say, and I chuckle at His mirth. He continues with a lift in His voice, though He is still unseen to my eyes. "You are my inheritance [Ephesians 1:18]! I rejoice in the ones my blood was shed for. I rejoice that my Father will receive His just reward and that I will receive mine [Revelation 22:12]. You are mine and I rejoice over you. You make my heart glad, child. I love you and am happy just being near you."

At His words, a warmth floods my being. I smile and think deeply on what He has just said. After a moment of reflection, I say, "It's funny how you feel the same way about me that I feel about you, Jesus. To think, you are excited and glad to be around *me*? Amazing. Simply amazing."

> I SIT IN HIS PRESENCE JUST PONDERING HIS RICH LOVE, ALLOWING UNSPOKEN THINGS TO BE COMMUNICATED BETWEEN US.

I sit in His presence just pondering His rich love, allowing unspoken things to be communicated between us. After a moment of silence I ask, "What do you want to say to me today, Lord? Anything else about anything else?"

At my request, a vision unfolds before my eyes. I am sitting under the tree—our tree—with Jesus. We are leaning against its obliging trunk. The Master has His arm casually around me. He gently squeezes me, pulls me close, and kisses me on the forehead as a father would his child. I smile as I watch this serene picture unfold. I cast my eyes to the timber that canopies over us, and all at once I remember, out loud, "This is the Tree of Life! This is where we sit! I have forgotten that."

I feel a prompting to study this tree again. I stand up and face the stunning structure. Jesus is smiling, still seated on the ground, looking up at me in approval as I place my hands on the bark and let my fingers quizzically peruse the rough texture. The crags and vales of the surface move under my hands like a rhythm that rises and falls. Its very existence feels like music to me. With a contented smile, I look back at Jesus and He returns my pleasure.

Jesus encourages me further. "Study it," He says.

I place my attention on the bark, peering intently at it. I suddenly see gold light streaming from deep inside it, peering out through its variegated surface. I draw my eye closer, peeking between its layers. As I lean in, I blink and am suddenly no longer outside of the tree, but find myself standing *inside* the midst of the trunk. Here a mystery finds me: it is not cramped or engulfed by darkness as one would imagine. I am not trapped immovably inside layers of fortified lumber. Instead, I find myself in a wide-open space filled with gold light all around, swirling and swirling slowly about me. The movement of light unfurls like ribbons delicately dancing in an unseen breeze. I stand with mouth agape in wonder as the exquisite dance moves around me. Soon, I focus my attention ahead of me and notice through the light a large, golden heart suspended before me. I draw closer to it and find it is beating and releasing dancing ribbons of light with every pulse. I am mesmerized as waves of power and love stream off of it. I close my eyes and let all of this light, power, and love flow into my body. Then, as quickly as I entered, I am back outside again with Jesus. I turn to Him with eyes wide in wonder and, after a moment of stunned silence, say the only word that can escape my mouth: "Wow."

With a look of wisdom warming His face, Jesus says, "Life is at the center of my heart. Life, true life, is only found in me [John 17:3]. And life will be fully manifested in you through love. You cannot receive my life without receiving my love [John 3:16]. And you are only full of life as you are full of my love. That's what you were feeling and receiving in the center of the tree—love—and that *is* life."

I throw myself into the arms of Jesus, embracing Him tightly. "It is good to be with you, Lord!"

Jesus reassures me. "You truly are mine, child," He says, rubbing my back gently.

The vision before me changes and I see us walking hand in hand across our garden, only now I am a child, no older than five or six years of age. My guileless eyes look up at Jesus and I ask, "What shall we do today, Lord?"

Smiling down at me with the love of the Father, gently swinging my hand, the Savior says, "Anything you want!"

Puzzled, I reply, "But, you are the Lord. You decide what to do and where to go."

Jesus picks me up and puts me on His hip. "It is my desire to give you the desires of your heart [Psalm 37:4]. You see, as you walk with me, you grow with me."

Jesus puts me back down beside Him and He begins to walk again, holding my hand. But I can see that I am growing older as we walk, for now I appear to be nine or ten years of age. The Lord continues, "This is friendship, child. To walk with me is to know my heart. You can be trusted with the storeroom of Heaven [Psalm 25:14]. It doesn't matter where you go or what you want to do. When you are my friend, your purposes are my purposes. Do you see this [John 15:14, 15]?"

Even though I know this kind of trust from the Lord only comes out of growing friendship with Him, His words still seem a bit daunting. Quizzically, I say, "You are saying you

"AS YOU CARRY MY HEART, MY LIFE INSIDE OF YOU, YOUR PULSE WILL BE MY PULSE. YOU WILL CHOOSE WHAT I CHOOSE. WE ARE ONE."

can trust me. You can trust my choices and decisions, right?"

This makes Jesus smile. "Yes," He says with an assurance. "As you carry my heart, my life inside of you, your pulse will be my pulse. You will choose what I choose. We are one. Melded together, melted down like precious metals mixed as one. True union. I can ask you what you want to do because you are full of my Spirit and He will always lead you. Do you trust this [Romans 6:5-9; Galatians 5:16]?"

My expression all but pales. "This is major, Jesus," I respond as the weight of His words lands upon me. I know what He is teaching me is an invitation that many believers will fail to enter due to their lack of *truly abiding* in Christ. I know this is an invitation with much responsibility and much honor. "This really is transformation, isn't it?" I ask with sobriety.

Softly, Jesus answers, "Yes, child. You see, I give you the keys of the kingdom. Whatever you bind on earth will be bound in Heaven. Whatever *you* loose on earth will be loosed in Heaven [Matthew 16:19]. Because you understand me, because you are my friend, you act and think like me. You do as I would do. You just know my heart, and we are made similar. So I give you freedom to choose as you are baptized in, dipped in, the power of my Spirit. It's amazing, yes?"

I can only nod in wonderment.

Still walking hand in hand with me, Jesus continues. "You are full of my light, even as the tree is full of light. You are planted as a tree among the woods [Song of Songs 2:3; Psalm 1:1-3]. You carry so much more than you realize inside of you. You have been given my authority on this earth. Learn to trust that and walk in that. See yourself as one who can make the right decisions, as the one who knows where my Spirit is moving. You must see this in yourself. Trust my working in you. Keep your eyes off of yourself, as I see your tendency even now to look at your weakness [Hebrews 12:1, 2; 2 Corinthians 12:9]. You won't find me by looking at your weakness, child. I am your *strength*. I am your glory. I am the one moving and working in you to enable and empower you. Never look at your self-limitations. When you do, the enemy will cloud your perspective. Keep your eyes on me."

"Wow. OK. It's all so . . . so . . . basic, isn't it, Lord?" I stutter in astonishment.

Still swinging my hand as He walks, the Lord smiles and says, "Truly, the life lived in me is simple [Matthew 11:30]. Man complicates it. But trust in who I am is simply that: trust. It boils down to knowing what I have said and keeping your eyes on me. Knowing that I am who I say I am *in you* upon this earth."

I shake my head in wonder. "Wow. It's amazing, Jesus." I notice now that, as He has been speaking and I have been listening, I am full grown.

Smiling, Jesus stops and turns to me, an understanding flowing between us as I realize my mature state. Then, He raises His brows and says, "The question remains: what do you want to do today?"

Returning His smile, I think for a moment and say, "Honestly, I want to go wherever you go. I want to keep a song in my heart as I go about my duties. That's good enough for me."

With a quick nod of approval, the Master says, "OK. Sounds good to me too!" He then continues to stroll with me.

Laughing, I say, "You're so funny, Jesus. Thanks for being my friend. I wouldn't tell anyone else I see you this way because it would sound too irreverent, but you're my buddy."

This extremely casual word doesn't even faze the Lord. "I know and I understand it. It's good to be companions, child. I like knowing that you can call me buddy. It carries meaning in your heart because I have placed it there [Proverbs 18:24; John 15:15]. I am your buddy. Do not let that phrase cause you to shudder. Yes, I am King, I am holy, but you can call me your closest companion—that is, a buddy! I am both!"

His words fill me with freedom as I understand that this holy, all-consuming fire, all-powerful God is the lover of my soul and the friend who sticks closer than a brother. I sigh in reverent contentment. "Yes, Lord. To the pure all things are pure [Titus 1:15]."

"Exactly."

Swinging our hands back and forth, I finish my time with Him saying, "OK. Let's have fun today singing together. I love you, Lord."

"And I love you too, child!"

THE SIMPLE SONG OF LOVE

Allowing the words of a song to move from mere words to conversation is an excellent way to take you into the unseen realm of the Father's heart. On another day I was singing along to the first CD I received from International House of Prayer in Kansas City. This ministry is best known for 24/7 prayer and worship going up for many years now in the spirit of the Tabernacle of David. Beyond that, however, they are known for singing the Word of God while they pray. Today they have digital streaming available all day and all night that allows you to join into the songs and intercession at any time, but back when they first began, the only way to listen to them at home was through old-fashioned compact discs. I listened over and over to that first CD, praying through Scriptures and being caught up in their spontaneous worship.

One day I sat down to pray and journal while listening to this album. As I sat singing a line birthed from their prayers that said, "Let the seed go deep, rooted and grounded in love," the image of an apple split open came to me. It was so vibrant and real in my mind's eye. I could see the apple as if it had been cut in two right before me. I sat looking at the white flesh inside, and right at the center of the apple was the hollow middle that held the seed. I wasn't sure if this image was my imagination or if it was from the Lord, but I knew it was worth exploring. I am so glad I did, for the Lord began to download His words into my spirit. With the vision of the apple before my eyes and the words from the song echoing in my heart, the Lord began speaking.

> "The seed is in the center of the apple. In the hollow center is the place of abundant seed, the place of multiplication, of one hundred-fold power. In the place, the hollow place where there is no flesh, my seed is planted [John 3:6]."

> I knew the Lord was speaking to me about the place where my flesh no longer exists—the place of the new life in Christ, the life of the Spirit that has set me free from the life of the fleshly nature. The Lord continued, "In the center of the flesh is the place of the seed."

> In saying this, I knew He was referring to the seat of my spirit-man at the center of my being.

> "In the center of your rest, of your refreshing, is the seed of multiplication. Out of one apple, if you were to plant a single seed, you would receive a hundred-fold return. The day is coming and now is at hand when my people will sow and receive abundance [Amos 9:13]. I am not calling my people, my bride, to a single moment of refreshing, but to a continual encounter to plant and receive, plant and receive, that which refreshes and delights the heart. I have given my bride the power of multiplied effort [Leviticus 26:8; Matthew

13:8, 9]. Deep in the flesh of my refreshed one, deep in the center of your being, is my love. This seed will multiply into many, many more seeds. The power of life inside you is truly amazing. One seed planted in your depths gives way to much more. One seed can root and go so deep that the apple becomes a mighty tree, giving birth to one tree after another [John 4:35]."

His words continue to rush over me. "My seed, my Word, planted in your heart is multiplying. I have made the illustration of the apple sliced open for you to see. The seed of my Word, my love, is hidden deep within. Only as the apple is cut in two can it be seen. Only my Word, which divides joint and marrow, soul and spirit, can get to the heart of a man or woman [Hebrews 4:12]. Deep within is the place of the seed. It is those who let the seed go deep who will be rooted in love [Ephesians 3:17]. They have ingested it, buried it deep within. It isn't sour—it is sweet. It is refreshing. It brings delight.

"There in the heart of the vessel is the power for many, many more truths, many, many more words, many, many more lives to be impacted. I release to you the gift of multiplication. The time of abundant harvest is at hand. What you plant in small form will spring forth to a mighty tree capable of feeding many [Matthew 13:31, 32]. Let my words divide you. Let my Spirit cut you open. Let the heart of your being be exposed.

"You are called to be a tree. Just as I bring you to my apple tree of refreshing, so are you to be a tree of refreshing to others [Song of Songs 2:3, 4; Psalm 92:12-14]. I have multiplied myself in you. Do not be afraid to be laid open in front of the hungry. Seek first my kingdom and everything else you need will be handed to you [Matthew 6:33]. I am what refreshes. I am in you, planted deep. My words, my promises, are planted deep. They have found good soil and have taken root. Do not be hasty in seeing the seed sprout forth [Ecclesiastes 3:11]. Just trust. I am producing in you a harvest. The principle is seen time and again in my Word. Trust me to do it in you."

PRAISE IS A WEAPON

One can never say enough about the power of praise and worship, about what it does to the atmosphere around us, about how it changes *us* from the inside out, and about how it moves the Father to act on our behalf. One day I found it easy to sing my praise to Him as I began getting ready for the day. I sat down to spend time with the Lord, and I found myself learning an awesome lesson about the song I had just been offering Him.

"Good morning, Lord! I am here for you today! I place myself at your throne of grace and come to you to hear and to obey. I love you, Lord. What do you want to share with me this morning? So many things are going through my mind, Father. Worship, songs, love for you, Spirit!"

As my heart speaks to the Father, I see a quick image of His finger touching the still waters of my heart, which causes a ripple effect that spreads across my soul. The ripples gently wash out to every part of my body. I hear the Father speak.

"My waves gently move the hindrances away," He says. "The ripples carry *out* what is not needed so what is in the center can come forth."

I understand as He says this that the center part of me is where my spirit lies. As He touches my spirit, it comes alive like rippling water. My spirit responds to Him from the inner-most part of me, and that response flushes out the distractions around me even as the rippling water carries away what once was there. I watch the image of the rippling water again and feel such praise welling up within.

"My soul longs for you, Lord. My shield. My song. My portion, you are."

No vision fills my eyes, but I hear Him say back to me, "I love you, daughter of Zion! Your praise to me is sweet. I have put a new song in your mouth, a new melody of praise [Psalm

40:3]. Sing it forth and let it rise!"

I rest in the moment, overcome in worship, letting my love song rise to the Lord. Time passes by in sweetness with joyous tears rolling down my cheeks as the song of worship overflows in response to the Father's touch upon my heart. After a while I settle into His presence, listening for anything His sweet voice might say. He gently begins.

"I wear your praise like a garment. No, my strength does not depend on your praise, for I am power. I am strong. But when my people praise me, it moves my arm of power on their behalf, and this excites me [Psalm 93:1; Isaiah 51:9; compare Matthew 21:16 with Psalm 8:2]! It is why I am here now! To move with and for my people! I am here for you and you are here for me; we move together. Your praise moves my hand; it moves my arms to act for you, to fight for you.

"See me clothed in the garments you have given me, dipped in blood, working vengeance on my enemies . . . coming up from Bozrah [Isaiah 63]." The imagery of Isaiah 63 fills my vision as I see the Lord draped in beautiful royal garments, dripping with the blood of my spiritual enemies, zealously shouting His victory for me, an indescribable love for me displayed in His vengeance. It is a fearsome thing to behold!

He continues. "I am able to act in mighty vengeance upon the enemy's camp because my people partner with my heart in worship and praise [Psalm 149]. They declare me as the Holy One of Israel and I am moved to act. The final battle of the last days will show forth my power *because* of the praise of my people, and I will arise in Zion like never before [Revelation 5:6-10]. My people will clothe me with strength—with the strength of their praise [Psalm 96:8]. 'Awake, awake, O arm of the Lord,' they will proclaim, and I will act [Isaiah 51:9]. Their song will stir my heart, will stir the garments I wear, and I will be moved from my place to where they are."

At His words, I see the praises of God's people rising up to the heavens like smoke rising from a fire, but somehow having a living nature, swirling around His glorious, holy throne where He is seated in His royal scarlet robe. The swirling praise begins to blow like a soft breeze upon the edge of His garment near His feet, just barely moving the hem. The praises of God's people continue, and the more the praises rise the more the winds blow upon Him. It stirs at His feet, then His legs, then reaches His waist, until, at last, He stands with arms extended like wings, eyes closed in holy ecstasy as the breath of His people fully engulfs Him with their praise!

"This is what I wait for," He roars, not with volume, but with authority. "I do it now, presently, every time you praise me. I am moved by the sound of your voice. As your voices arise in worship, it is the cry of my heart to reply in power and mercy and strength [Psalm 91:15]. I will work against those who come against you as you praise and as you worship. As you lift me up, I am filled with the songs of Heaven, I am filled with the power of your love, and I am able to move for you and through you. Your silence hinders my hands. It binds them up from releasing vengeance and blessings on your behalf [Ezekiel 22:30, 31]. But praise is the weapon you are given to release the things of Heaven upon the earth. You will fight best when you fight with the song of the redeemed on your lips. You are called to battle in this way, even today, for the souls of the lost ones. You move me when you declare that I alone am God, I alone can save them. I will crush Satan under your feet as you lift me up and declare I am God [Romans 16:20]. You move me, child. You move me, my bride. I fight for you."

Once again, the image of Isaiah 63 unfolds before me: the holy Lord zealous in victory and love for His bride. "Lord," I say, "I see you dipped in blood, the garments you wear covered in blood, as Isaiah declares in chapter 63."

I hear Him declare, "Yes, I am fighting for you even now [Deuteronomy 20:4]. Your praise is a surge of energy in the heavens. Like a bomb that goes off and causes shock waves, so is your praise."

His words paint the image of a singular person offering praise to the Lord. The simple praise sends off a massive shock wave of light that is released from the inner man, flooding the landscape with a luminous power in every direction and reaching into the heavens. Jesus breaks in: "The praise of one of my children causes major shaking in the heavenly realm. How much more so the joined praises of my body? It is an unstoppable force, and it will not be moved from the earth. This is the power that will be released in the last-day army. The power of united praise and purpose which will cause the shaking in the heavens and cause the shaking in the earth [Isaiah 42:8-13]. 'Open your mouth and I will fill it,' says the Lord! 'I will do a new thing. Once again I will shake everything that can be shaken and I will do it through the mouths of my people in song, in praise, in prayer. It will be done,' says the Lord [Haggai 2:6, 7; Revelation 19]!"

'OPEN YOUR MOUTH AND I WILL FILL IT,' SAYS THE LORD! 'I WILL DO A NEW THING. ONCE AGAIN I WILL SHAKE EVERYTHING THAT CAN BE SHAKEN.

His words cause my heart to tremble with anticipation as His great authority crashes against me. In raptured praise I cry, "Then I release my song of praise to you today! I will not look to the left or to the right, but will keep my praise on you! Oh Lord, my Lord!" I once again look upon the image of the child of God offering praise that begins a wave of power extending all around Him. In this moment, I notice, "The shock wave of praise in the heavens is similar to the ripple of water I saw in my heart at the beginning of our time together today. This is a good word, God."

I hear the Lord respond. "What appears to you as a gentle ripple can appear to me as crashing waves. The spiritual eye sees differently. The spiritual eye *lives* differently. Do not discredit even the smallest thanks, even the smallest praise offered, child. In the heavenlies, it is much more."

> "THE SPIRITUAL EYE SEES DIFFERENTLY. THE SPIRITUAL EYE *LIVES* DIFFERENTLY. DO NOT DISCREDIT EVEN THE SMALLEST THANKS, EVEN THE SMALLEST PRAISE OFFERED, CHILD."

The lessons about the Tree of Life and the apple were both unique in that they started with a song and took me into an entirely different revelation. The Lord was teaching me so much more than how to use song to hear Him speak. He was teaching me truths of His kingdom! He was teaching me how to catch glimpses in understanding who He is, and that is the most powerful revelation one can ever receive. And it all began with a simple song of love. A simple song of praise.

We must never let anything stop our praise! All the doubt the enemy throws at us, all the questions of "Did God really say?" and "Are you really a child of God?" are targeted at our praise because Satan sees what we cannot see: the unmatched power that is released when God's people respond with faith in praise to their Father.

I believe there is a day coming when the confidence of God's people in who He is and who they are will culminate in a praise so united that Christ cannot help but split the skies in return for His beloved bride. Until that day, every simple song, every simple praise is causing the enemy to take flight. So let your song rise and invite the Spirit to teach you and commune with your heart in every melody offered. Be encouraged, O bride of Christ—your song of love matters more than you know!

CHAPTER CONFIDENCE KEYS: HOW TO HEAR GOD'S VOICE

1. Bring your song to the Lord. Many people sing to God in church or in the car, but the song on your heart is meant to be so much more. It is meant to be a lovely exchange of poetry between you and your Maker. If you aren't naturally musical, it's OK! Simply bring one of your favorite songs to Jesus by singing or reciting phrases slowly to Him a phrase at a time. Think about the words. Roll them over in your mind, pausing on the phrases that seem to speak to you most. Chances are you are feeling "more life" in certain phrases because it is an invitation to you to converse with the Lord about the truths found there. Use your journal to write down what you feel He is saying to you through the song. You will be surprised at how much truth waits for you there!

2. Music is a great way to silence the analytical side of our mind. If you are having a hard time connecting with God in prayer because of distractions or worry, tune in one of your favorite worship songs. Music is scientifically proven to connect your head with the intuitive side of your heart. It is also biblical. When Elisha needed to hear from God in 2 Kings 3, he called for a musician (2 Kings 3:15). As the music played, he was able to hear from the Lord. It will work for you too!

CHAPTER CONFIDENCE KEYS: KNOWING WHO YOU ARE IN GOD

1. You are given the invitation to become a true friend of God. This isn't an invitation for a special select few. It is for anyone who will walk and talk with Jesus in day-to-day life. By choosing simple conversation throughout the day, you are actually stepping into maturity in your friendship with God. Without forcing it or working up a sweat, your friendship is growing. He has sent you the invitation and made it easy for you to accept. Just love Him

and spend time with Him and you will see your friendship with God grow.

2. Satan wants nothing more than to keep you looking at your own limitations and weakness. God wants nothing more than for you to look to His perfect love, strength, and power. The greatest position a child of God can ever find themselves in is not one of soul-searching but of Savior-seeking! Gaze upon Him! Look to Him! You will never be strong enough or good enough to earn a thing from Him. Even your maturing process and growing friendship comes as you focus on who He is, not on who you are. This is to truly fear Him: to know that He is everything you need and that He lavishly pours out goodness on the one who humbly seeks Him as their all in all. Understand that, in Him, you lack no good thing (Psalm 34:9). Let your emptiness awaken confidence that He will fill you with everything you need for life and godliness (2 Peter 1:3).

3. Your praise is powerful! No matter how broken or how feeble it may seem to you, your praise causes the enemy to flee. Even if all you can offer God is the whisper of His name, know that the smallest praise sends off a spiritual nuclear explosion that you cannot see. This is the power of your position in Christ. Let the image burn in your heart.

Chapter 7

LESSONS FROM THE CHAIN BREAKER

My time with the Lord was truly freeing my heart from fear and condemnation. But it wasn't always easy. I had been trained through religion to be so fearful of sin, to be so fearful of failing God, that even in the midst of my increasing courage, I found myself in old thinking patterns of self-condemnation and anxiety. As I grew in confidence in hearing His voice, the Lord began to show me these areas of fear in my spirit. He began to teach me how deeply fear roots itself inside of His people in the name of religion, in the name of doctrine, and in the name of being "well-grounded." Since I was raised in church, I had much to *unlearn* as I grew in confidence. In order for me to learn how He saw me as His child, He had to break off many lies that I had unwittingly been taught: lies about my performance being a factor of receiving His love, lies about my sin keeping me from approaching Him, lies about how He feels about me in my weakness, and more.

As I was growing in confidence in hearing God speak, I was also slowly finding myself less concerned about people's opinions of me.

I WAS ALSO GROWING IN CONFIDENCE IN BEING HIS CHILD. IN HEARING HIS VOICE I WAS FINDING MY IDENTITY.

It was an amazing freedom taking over my heart! Like most people, insecurity was my childhood friend and lifelong acquaintance. It was just as natural for me to fear people's opinions of me as it was to fear a gigantic spider crawling across my face. As I grew in believing I could hear His voice, however, I was also growing in confidence in being His child. In short, in hearing His voice I was finding my identity.

I am more and more convinced that as we approach Jesus for *yada time*, it is impossible for us to not be changed from our encounter. Like the bridegroom He is, Jesus is zealous for His bride to be free from anything that hinders our pursuit of Him. And it's not just the pursuit of Him He's after: He is after us simply being free for freedom's sake. Galatians 5:1 says (NIV), "It is for freedom that Christ has set you free." He didn't set you free to be a workhorse for Him. He didn't set you free even simply for the reason of loving Him with everything you have. That's your *choice* to give—*you* are the one who chooses what to do with the freedom He has given you. He simply sets you free trusting that when you awaken to the freedom He has given you, you won't be able to do anything but love Him with every fiber of your being in return. He wants each and every one of us to be not only free from sin, but also free from insecurities, fears, wounds, and unhealthy emotions. To quote Galatians 5:1 in *The Passion Translation*, Jesus wants us, "not partially, but completely and wonderfully free!"

FREE FROM PRIDE

All of this exposure to God's love in my prayer time was a bit daunting. I was concerned about levels of unseen pride in my life, especially as I grew in confidence in hearing His voice. I knew it would be too easy to hear what I wanted to hear when I journaled if my heart was full of pride. This thought alarmed me, so I took it directly to the Lord. I simply prayed.

"Wash me in humility, precious King. Only you can keep me from stumbling in the pride of men, the pride of my own heart. I need you to keep me in the place of humility. I need you, Spirit, to show me the traps of my own pride. Here I come and bow, humbling myself like I know how. Help me hear only what you want me to hear. Help me not make up things. Help me trust. What do you want to speak to me? I lay my mind before you, Jesus. Sweet Spirit, come. Immerse me in you."

I waited quietly, expecting vision to fill my imagination. Instead, I immediately heard His voice on my heart: "Trust is a gift, a present, that I put in you."

INSTEAD, I IMMEDIATELY HEARD HIS VOICE ON MY HEART: "TRUST IS A GIFT, A PRESENT, THAT I PUT IN YOU."

As He spoke these words, I saw a large white gift box before my eyes, tied cheerfully in a bright red, oversized ribbon. He continued, "Trust is a present that is for you *and* for me. In this place of trust, this present, you are free." I next saw myself *inside* of this massive gift box called Trust, white light engulfing me all around, eyes closed in worship with a contented smile on my face, arms wide open in abandoned love for God.

The Lord continued. "You are guarded by trust on all sides. You are kept from the evil one [Psalm 91]. You are kept from pride. See, your eyes are closed in abandoned worship in this gift of trust. It is a gift to my bride—one that she must learn to utilize. She is crippled without it. You are meant to live in this gift."

The irony hit me how I had often complained about being trapped in a box of stifling religion. Now I saw myself in a box where I looked totally and completely free!

Jesus explained it all. "*This* box is the box you are meant to be in. It opens up wide to new levels of praise and revelations of my kingdom [2 Samuel 22:3, 4; Proverbs 3:5]. Do not let fear hinder you. You want to fear failing me, your flesh wants to dress up your fear of failing me in a holy garment. But understand this: you are not called to fear [2 Timothy 1:7; 1 John 4:18]. Fear of *me* is a place of trust and belonging. *Do not fear your pride—crucify it. Crucify it in worship. Crucify it in trust and peace* [Romans 6:1-11; Galatians 2:20; Colossians 3:1-6]. If it is crucified, it is dead. You cannot fear what is dead. It cannot harm you.

"You must not boast in this, of course. For you cannot boast in the power of the cross for yourself. The power of the cross is *mine* . . . and I make the way for you to come to it. You boast in my cross, not your own [Galatians 6:14]. Pride is destructive, but do not fear it: Fear me. There is a vast difference here. I will teach you to trust me more. If you fear pride, you give it too much credit. Yes, many have fallen here before. Many have been caught in its trap [Proverbs 8:13, 11:2; 1 Timothy 3:6]. But their eyes were not directed to the *fear of me*. I alone can keep you from this trap. Take my hand and trust. If you don't leave this place, this gift, this place of trust and reliance on me as your supplier of *all* things, then you will not fall. Come to me. Learn from me my humility and you will stand [John 6:53-55; Philippians 2:5-11].

> "IF YOU COME TO THE CROSS DAILY AND KEEP WATCH ON YOUR HEART, THEN YOU DO WELL. WHAT IS THERE TO FEAR IN YOU WHEN YOU ARE AT THE CROSS DAILY?"

"If you come to the cross daily and keep watch on your heart, then you do well. What is there to fear in you when you are at the cross daily? There is nothing to fear, for here in this place

I am in you. But you must come. Stay in this place of trust. Do not dress it up in false humility. This is what the devil wants to do: to make you think you are worthless and in danger of falling. This lifestyle will never produce the *life* of me in you. It has trapped and paralyzed the bride for years. It is a form of fearing man: fearing *yourself*. Do not look at self. Look at me" [Genesis 3:6-8; 1 John 2:16]."

FREE FROM LEGALISM

During a particular season, I was awakening to the truth of His grace in entirely new ways. I was watching chains of legalism fall off of my life, bringing me into a freedom that was grounding me deeper. The truth between the tensions was astounding: I was more grounded but freer than ever before! As often is the case in my life, this freedom made me pause in fear. What if I was wrong? What if I was not hearing correctly? What if I was going into error?

I brought these worries to the Lord one day, feeling the prison walls of legalism and fear crouching in, and once again found very little vision, but tons of conversation. Jesus spoke.

"Child, you are free from this prison. My blood dissolves the lock. I destroyed the chains, the bars that held you back in your pursuit and understanding of me. Sin is the enemy, but it does not have dominion over you [Romans 6:14]. It does not have dominion over my people. People have feared sin, they have feared my wrath. My people, they have not understood justice and mercy; they have not understood freedom's song. Paul and Silas understood it."

At this, I see an image of a filthy, dank prison cell built underground with ancient stones, mossy and slimy in appearance. To the right, Paul and Silas are chained to a wall, wrists and ankles tethered in iron. They are both bleeding and oozing from a beating received on their backs. Sweat glistens on their brow, mingled with black patches of dirt and muck from their ordeal of being thrown to the ground. Here they sit, tethered and wounded in pitch-black night. (For a fuller version of this, see Acts 16:16-34.)

"They were truly free," Jesus says. "But even these great men of faith had to learn what was theirs by right and access it. Do not think that you are so far removed from the lessons they had to learn. Paul had much to *relearn*. He had things He had to forget, child [Philippians 3:1-16; Galatians 1:13–2:2]! He is no different than you in all of the reshaping and reforming of his mind-sets. But, in an instant, I can shake false ideas and establish truth [2 Corinthians 4:3-6]. This is how it is for you and how it was for Paul. In an instant, I open the door and show you the way to freedom, but there is still the process of you walking down the hallways past the barred windows and doors, past the concrete embankments and imprisonments, into freedom, into the free air. Often, when people enter the courtyard of freedom for the first time, they run back inside to what they've known [Galatians 5:1]. The bars and walls seem safer. They are afraid that without any boundaries they will run into a ditch, that they won't see where they are going. Before, they were always kept under guard [Galatians 3:23], but out in freedom's valley there is no guard and suddenly they feel afraid. I am patient with these, though, daughter. You've been there before. You entered back into a prison that had an open door."

At His words, I see an image of a prison cell again, only this time it is well lit and the door is open. Chains lie on the floor, obviously used before, but now no longer holding their captive. I see myself walking willingly into this little cell. I am not sad or lonely in appearance. No, I am determined to return to this place. I sit down next to the chains in this open cell. I am dressed in flowing white garments.

"You thought that this place was holy. But I met you here, daughter. I fed you even in the middle of this law-based prison."

I see Jesus enter the cell with me. He is dressed plainly, not beautifully as I am. Patiently and kindly, He sits down next to me, laying open a picnic basket, handing me delicious fare to enjoy. He is relaxed with me, leaning on one elbow, smiling and chatting like an old friend. In any other location it would have been a serene image to view, but the contrast of such serenity in a prison is not lost as I watch the image move.

The Lord continues, "But here I came to you and appeared to you as a kind pauper, a poor caretaker, a kind soul."

I understand as He speaks that, for many years, I considered Him as a kind jailer, someone who was courteous and loving, but still in charge of keeping me in prison.

> I UNDERSTAND AS HE SPEAKS THAT, FOR MANY YEARS, I CONSIDERED HIM AS A KIND JAILER, SOMEONE WHO WAS COURTEOUS AND LOVING, BUT STILL IN CHARGE OF KEEPING ME IN PRISON.

"I am gentle with those who are still held back by law mentalities," He continues. "I am gentle with them to draw them back out into freedom's air [Galatians 4:1-7]. Many will hear freedom's songs echoing in from the outside; they will hear it and think that it is error. These will often retreat farther into the prison for safekeeping—a separation from what they think is false teaching. But even these, child, I come to over and over to feed them with my love, my body, my blood. I desire to woo them out into the open air.

"Many are being led there and have no idea. Like you, child. You exited out and it was as if you saw for the first time [John 3:3]. Even though you had known me and experienced my love, when you truly found freedom was when you had the veil lifted from your eyes. And *then* you came into freedom [2 Corinthians 3:12-18]."

I see myself now standing with Jesus in a wide-open field of waving grass and wildflowers. I have gone from a tiny prison cell into endless territory!

Jesus stands beside me in this vast green field. He is no longer clothed in meager garments but in a beautiful white robe with a golden crown on His head. He says, "It was as if the ceiling was removed . . . and it was. Out here in freedom, you can see me as I truly am: not as a pauper or an unjust God, but as the kind King who gives all to His children. I am a most benevolent ruler! Now, the world is yours [Romans 8:32]. It's all yours and you are unafraid. You can run free without fear of falling because I am your life, the life inside you. I fill up your lungs. I grace your frame with my presence, with my very existence. You are free indeed [John 8:34-36]. Only as you trust this finished work can you run free. As soon as you start wondering about your feet, you will trip. When your eyes get off of me and onto your own walk, you often fall [Hebrews 12:1, 2]. But freedom is natural. It's like the air you breathe, like the space all around you. You don't have to worry about where to step: I am with you and in you. You've got all the freedom available to you to run and play and climb in."

"YOU CAN RUN FREE WITHOUT FEAR OF FALLING BECAUSE I AM YOUR LIFE, THE LIFE INSIDE YOU. I FILL UP YOUR LUNGS."

I cannot help but spin and laugh in the freedom fields I am standing in. I am next to the King who has given me all things to enjoy! All life! All freedom! All of who He is is given to me!

Jesus laughs. "What you're learning is right. I'm opening up more and more to you, child. Just come and run with me. Play with me in this field of freedom. I'm about to teach you new things in the area of my Spirit that you've not known, that you could not know behind prison doors of law and legalism. You cannot learn my heights when your eyes are set on yourself. *You* cannot fly—but I can." A smile spreads across His face, and He continues. "The ways of my Spirit are always to fly. That's why I will mount you up like an eagle [Isaiah 40:30, 31]. I will take you higher because you are free. You're not tethered and bound. You are free to go higher, to spread your wings out farther. People are so afraid of failing when they first step out . . . but I am with you. What you call failing, I often do not. There is grace upon grace upon you because I am in you and with you. Let's take another leap together, child! Let's soar on new heights!"

FREE TO BE YOURSELF

No man ever walked freer than Jesus. No other man heard the Father more clearly, and no other man was more confident in his sonship. I knew freedom to be yourself was tied to the revelation of sonship that Christ understood. But another thought was being revealed to me as I pondered Christ's nature: no other man was freer from other people's opinions (John 2:24, 25)! He was not swayed by politics or emotions. He was not swayed by public opinion or the size of the crowd that followed Him. He was secure and unwavering in His identity as God's Son. Pondering this beautiful nature, I sat one day to talk to Him about it.

"Thank you, Lord. You are so awesome. You are so . . . *you*. You are truly true to yourself and your nature. You didn't care what others thought about you, yet you were totally concerned about others. Oh, Jesus! I want to be like that! Free from the fear of man but free to love them without bars! Oh, let it be in me! This is what freedom looks like!"

Immediately, the Lord answers. "Child, this revelation has your heart because it is a high calling, and it is one you are called to. Oh, the joy of knowing you see it, child! I want all of my children to see this great invitation! True freedom comes to us when we walk in a way where we do not fear man's opinions of us [Matthew 10:26, 28]. This comes, however, from having a firm foundation in ourselves—confidence in who we are in God alone. Awakening to this is vital for the church in this hour, as I have told you, dear. A firm foundation in understanding who we are as individuals in the body is vital to walk in the freedom of the Lord [1 Corinthians 12]. Knowing who we are awakens us to walk before His eyes, to live before His gaze."

I am a bit confused by the grammatical point of view Jesus is using. I quizzically say, "Jesus, you don't usually talk like this, in the first person plural. In fact, I don't believe I have ever heard you say, '*we* do not fear,' '*we* as individuals,' and so on. Are you referring to the Father as Lord? Are you talking about you and me in the 'we'—because that doesn't make sense. Am I hearing right?"

"I am speaking to you as one who has had to learn to walk the walk of faith in God alone. I, fully human, had to learn to live before *His* eyes [Luke 2:30]. This comes in knowing who I am. In knowing who I am."

As He speaks, the Scripture and scene from John 13:1-5 opens before me. The passage says:

> *Now before the feast of the Passover, when Jesus knew that his hour had come that He should depart from the world to the Father, having loved His own who were in the world, He loved them to the end. And supper being ended, the devil had already put it into the heart of Judas Iscariot to betray Him.* **Jesus, knowing that the Father had given all things into His hands and that He had come from God and was going to God,** *rose from supper and laid aside His garments, took a towel and girded Himself . . . and began to wash the disciples' feet* (NKJV; author's note: emphasis is mine).

Jesus, knowing my thoughts, says, "Even as your heart is

thinking of John's account in the upper room [John 13:1-4], I knew who I was and knew where I was going. This freed me, then, to serve men because I was not connected to them for my identity. I was connected to them in service and love. Child, if you can learn your identity in me, you will be free to love and serve."

The revelation is just so pure I cannot help but weep. Tears stream down my cheeks as the Master continues.

"Child, I understood that true life was in me [John 5:26]. I *had* to be myself! I had no other choice if I wanted to save the world. I had to be true to my calling, true to my purpose and created purpose on earth. True freedom for others begins here: when we are true to our redeemed selves [1 Corinthians 7:17, 20]. The one who fears, who even fears man's opinions and nature, has not been perfected in love [1 John 4:18]. Love begins at the foundations of our calling, in knowing who we are created to be in our purpose on earth. If we do not know this, child, we will be looking to others to define us and our calling."

"Makes sense."

"To know your calling is to know yourself," Jesus continues. "And this is freedom, child, to truly be *you* as you are created to be [Colossians 3:23, 24]. Yes, apart from me you have no good thing. But 'you in me' *is* your new nature [2 Corinthians 5:17]! So, what does it look like? What are you created for? Finding it and doing it—this is freedom! Only *then* will you love rightly, for only then will you not be swayed by man's opinions of you. If you can be swayed in your calling based upon man's approval or disapproval, then you are not true to yourself—your redeemed self—and you are not loving them rightly, for it is shifting sand that changes with the tide of opinion."

Amazed, I say, "That makes sense too! Wow. I just feel this, Jesus. Freedom from fear of man and freedom to love are so hand in hand—like I've never realized!"

Although I had only seen the image from John 13 before me as I journaled, I just knew the Lord was smiling as He says, "You are created to bring salvation to the world as I was created to bring it, child [Mark 16:15]. You are called to take up your cross and die daily, to lay your life down for the brethren, to let your light shine [Matthew 16:24; 1 John 3:16]. Yes, I paid the price, but you are just as much witnesses to the Father on the earth as I was [1 John 4:17, 5:1-13]. You are called to be *life* to the dying around you. *My* life is in you, so you must be true to *yourself* too! Do you see this? You are created to walk in freedom as a dead man who now lives in me [Galatians 2:20]! You show *me*. You show my love and light! Yes, you reveal salvation, child! You are not the Savior—but you *are* a bringer of salvation [2 Corinthians 5:18-20]. Be true to yourself, child. Be true and you will be truth, life, and light to the lost and to the body around you. Yes, it is reliance on the Father! Dependence on the Spirit! But this *is in you*, child! Do not doubt! You are *made* to dwell with me and I in you [Ephesians 2:4-6]. This is your true self. Let the expression of it shine forth for all to see! Know that I am the life inside of you, enabling you to be yourself, to live above the opinions of man and to now walk in love like each one is the only one in the room."

Pondering His words, I reply, "This is what you are beginning in me, isn't it? You've been doing the first—the freeing me from man's opinions—but now you are awakening me to the latter: the ability to love each one in the room."

"Yes, daughter and child. You are awakening to this. Let me have my perfect work in you and you will have kindness like you are longing for, goodness like you've never known. You will love freely because you will be living free from man's grasp and influence. Yet you will be influenced by love."

In joyful revelation, I sigh, "That is *soo* good, Lord! I love it!"

"And I love you, daughter of Zion," I hear Him reply in warm affection. "You are called to this, but I will be the one who lights the flame. You just come and stand before my breeze with hands open and heart open and I will fan it into flame each day."

"Thank you, Lord."

FREE FOR FELLOWSHIP

On another occasion, I found the Lord speaking to me in an endless flow. By faith, I wrote down all that I believed He was saying; I was fascinated by what I heard Him speaking. I sat down and prayed.

"It has been a while since I have come in this fashion. I realize how key it is to journal with you, Lord, for I have missed you. I have felt less connected to your heart. I desire your beauty, Lord. Come and kiss me with your word, Jesus. I commit my heart, my eyes, my imagination to see. What would you like to speak to me this morning? Come, Holy Spirit."

As I wait in His presence, I hear the Lord impress His words upon me. "Let me look upon your face, Beloved, for your face is sweet [Song of Songs 3:14]. I desire truth in the innermost parts of your being, for it is here that I redecorate your frame, the secret eternal parts of you. I desire to look deep into you and remove all that hinders my fiery love from burning brightly [John 15:1-11; Philippians 1:6]. It is here where I dwell in fullness. It is here that I gaze upon your beauty."

"I don't understand, Lord," I confess. "You gaze upon *me* from the inside out?"

The Lord begins to explain His heart in a flood of knowledge. "I see those things that are not yet and call them out [Romans 4:17]. I see the inside. Because I desire truth in your being, I speak truth to you. I see it take root and form long before you do. I see what it will become: a strong tree with branches high and roots going deep. This is our tree that I plant deep inside of you: my truth, my words, my ways [Psalm 1:1-3]. It is here that I can speak comfort to you under the canopy of my truth. It is here that I declare who you are before me. I see the hidden things long before they are even born. I see the manifestation before you do.

"IT IS HERE THAT I DECLARE WHO YOU ARE BEFORE ME. I SEE THE HIDDEN THINGS LONG BEFORE THEY ARE EVEN BORN."

"Man truly looks at the outward appearance, but I see the heart. It is here in your heart that is dedicated to me where I declare your beauty. Yes, even in weakness, even in the little moves, I see your beauty—and I declare you are beautiful, child. You are lovely. You are mine. You are fair, my sister, my dove, even as I have declared it [Song of Songs 1:15, 5:1]! This is not simply my opinion. This is my declaration! I declare and it will be! What can stop my declaration? My word is living and active, ever producing what I declare it to be [Isaiah 55:10, 11]. You shall live and not die. You shall grow and not shrink. You shall manifest my beauty. These are things that I have declared from the inside of you, the deepest parts of you.

"Because you open yourself up to my Spirit, I can have free reign to declare and act in you. Yes, my Word is living, but it is also active [Hebrews 4:12]. This means I am moving in you to accomplish my Father's good will. I am the one who works among the garden. I am the one who plants and builds up. I am He who declares life to your roots and causes the rain of my Spirit to fall fresh down upon you. I bring the sunshine. I bring the light. I bring the wind. I bring the growth [John 15:1-5]. It is all for my glory! You are my glorious creation! I hold you up high for all the world to see, saying, 'This is my creation! This is the one that I love! This is my one and only!' You are my bride, child. You are my heart's song. It is this that you were created for—to be loved and to be sung over. It is my delight to see in you the deepest truth, that you are forever mine, forever lovely, forever united with my heart [Romans 8:31-39]."

I am so overcome by His words that I have to catch my breath. Pausing and pondering for a while, I finally find the strength to say, "I did not expect such lovely things from you this morning. I am so task-oriented. I thought for sure you would give me instructions."

"Your instruction is this: love me and let me love you!" He says. "Rest in me and let me rest in you. Sometimes the greatest thing you can do is rest [Hebrews 4:1-12]. If you will just play with me, sit with me—sometimes this is the greatest form of accomplishment you can achieve. When the world is pulling you every which direction, sometimes the victory is found in denying its pull, in sitting and resting with a smile on your face [Mark 1:35]. This is victory at its finest, child! You, embracing the opposite of what the world would pull on you. See how it is worship? See how it is powerful in action?"

"COME TO ME, AS I HAVE INSTRUCTED, LIKE A CHILD CASTING OFF RESTRAINT. PUT AWAY YOUR BIG-GIRL CLOTHES— YOUR ATTITUDE OF DUTY—AND SIMPLY BE MY FRIEND."

Chuckling to myself, I say, "Yes, Lord. I do see."

The Lord continues. "Come to me and I will give you rest [Matthew 11:28-30]. Come to me, as I have instructed, like a child casting off restraint. Put away your big-girl clothes—your attitude of duty—and simply be my friend. Rest in this. You want to carry my presence all day and mourn because you feel like you are losing it. Child, this is where it is *found*. In total assurance of faith that I am who I say I am and that you are who I have declared you to be [2 Corinthians 5:17]. Let this be what rests on your heart.

"I will help you in your duty the best when I am the One who rests upon your heart like a smile on your face. I will direct your prayers and scheduled prayer time. But do not get into the habit of thinking it is a checklist of accomplishments. I know you long to honor me in the secret place by bringing the needs of the body before me [Galatians 6:2]. I appreciate that hunger and drive. I will direct it. But do not turn on a mode that says, 'This is prayer time.' You abide in me by staying in me. Resting as a child. Take off responsibility as you know and understand it and just be with me. Just come to me as a child comes before her daddy. Be *this* person and you will be free in me, abiding all day continually" [Galatians 5:1; John 15].

"OK, Lord," I respond. "I can see where I've picked up some old habits of duty. Forgive me. I come to you for nothing else but to reflect on you today. Thank you, Lord. I love you."

FREE FROM GUILT

On another occasion I had been very busy helping my sister move into her new home, helping hang pictures and rearrange furniture while also watching her children while she was at work. I originally had grand plans of spending time with the Lord the week I was with my sister, but instead found myself busier than expected. Therefore, I spent very little time in extended prayer and was feeling guilty because of this. I was eager to get into His presence but also a bit afraid to receive correction for what I thought was failure to pray enough. Timidly, I came to the Lord in prayer.

"Good morning, Lord. Your Word has been sweet today. It is good to be back in a routine with you. It seems, Lord, that I keep falling at spending time with you when I do not have a routine. I hated not being with you this past week in union. Too busy and too many people around. Yuck. It's hard not being connected to you. I do ask for forgiveness, Lord, for neglecting time with you this past week. I receive cleansing from your blood and strength to stand before you now in confidence. Not by works but by faith in you who have called and cleansed me. Now, what would you like to speak to me today, dear Savior?"

As usual, the Lord visited me in overwhelming kindness. "Just come closer, daughter. Come and let my beauty, my glory, flood you now. Feel my love swallow you like waters in the open sea. You saw the sea this week. I took you to the waters physically. Let now your mind see the vast ocean. It is a drop of my love for you, of my cleansing for you. My sanctification for you is mightier, deeper, longer than any ocean. My work in you is a deep work because my love for you is a deep love. You do not start over when you've had a bad week of devotion time. You do not go back to square one as one who is punished in the corner and kicked off the team. You are forever my bride. My forever child. Nothing can separate you from my love. When I said 'nothing,' I meant *nothing*—not your plans to follow after me that fail. Not your plans to hear me more that never saw fruition. All of the plans you had for this past week that the enemy wants you to feel condemnation about: none of it separates you from my love.

"You asked for cleansing? You've got it: body and soul. It is that simple. My love for you is not a barometer, not something that changes with the seasons and conditions of life. It is a constant. The constant of life. I love the broken and the unlovely like they are my own flesh and blood. I love the holy and the blameless the same. Oh, I love you, my child. I'm proud of you for wanting me. I will help you find me more because you have set your heart on me. You desire me, and oh, I am moved. You want me and I want you. Do you know there are many who are not grieved when they go on vacation and don't get time with me? You are grieved because you love me. You were moved in lovesickness. Oh, how this makes my heart glad. I want to be wanted, child.

That deep desire for acceptance and love inside of you and all mankind is a character trait of my heart. I, too, desire to be loved, chosen, and wanted. It's not an insecurity in me like it is in you."

My precious moment was abruptly interrupted when my cat, Mallory, jumped on my lap, startling me and bringing back to the present. Laughing, I pet her and loved on her until she had had her fill and went her way in independent catlike fashion. I turned my attention again to prayer, smiling. "Lord, my cat just totally got in on our time together!"

Immediately, I hear Him speak. "Let me highlight what just happened to you now. This is how true love works. Mallory missed you, but now she is happy to be near you with exceeding joy! Why? Because she knows you love her and she loves you. You hated being gone from her and she hated you being gone. But now there is great rejoicing in your union. It is the same with you, child, when you get busy and don't spend the time with me like you want to. Yes, it is best, the better part, to stay in union with me even when your schedule is altered. This takes practice and time to learn. I will help you do this more and more, so do not worry. I will be with you to teach you how to abide in union with me even when life is hectic and out of sync.

"But, my child, it was one week of less time together. I do not discount your love because of this. But I do allow your lovesickness to be poured out. Because I know you love me and because you know I love you, we are able to get together today and greatly rejoice in our union. If your confidence in me was shallow, then there would be fear. See how you've overcome so much in this area!"

He was right. I had overcome a lot of condemnation and fear in our time together. "Yes, Lord," I respond. "Because of your love and my growing understanding of it, I am confident. I am cleansed and forgiven and I know it. And this brings such emotion to my heart."

"Yes, you have learned how to run back into my arms with confidence," Jesus says. "This is what I desire for all my children. I place a crown on your head. You run back to this rightful position because it is yours. You might not have felt the royal authority of being the King's daughter this week, but it was always yours. I do not take back my gifts, child. You are forever mine. You are forever the King's kid. You sense this now. Oh, let this confidence swell over you again."

Tears begin to fall as I rest in the ever-faithful love of God. With eyes stretched out to receive, I whisper, "Lord, now I will sit and just worship. Thank you for love that is not shaken and moved."

It is amazing how patterns of fear, unhealthy self-examination, and doubt can creep in, especially for those who have a religious upbringing. In learning to step out in faith and love and in believing I am hearing God's voice, I find that these patterns are slowly unwinding due to the freedom in which I am growing. When I walk through seasons of busyness or stress, it can become especially easy to find myself distracted. Therefore, if I am not rooted in love, I can easily come under condemnation for not "measuring up" to the spiritual goals I have set for myself—goals, may I add, that Jesus never set for me.

But because of the revelation of His grace, His goodness, and His zeal for my heart, these models of self-focused, legalistic behavior that were once so natural to me are now becoming more and more recognizable for what they really are: chains of bondage that Christ never gave me.

CHAPTER CONFIDENCE KEYS: HOW TO HEAR GOD'S VOICE

1. Bring your everything to the Lord—this means bring the doubts, the fears, the confusion that may creep into your heart. Ask Him to reveal to you what is religious in nature; what lie you have

believed as truth; what "good thing" you need to let go of for the "best thing," called freedom. He is not offended by your questions, doubts, or fears. Bring them to Him. Trust that He will speak in such a way that you will be freer than ever before.

2. Trust that the Lord will never lead you into bondage. He will never lead you into darkness. Take a good hard look at your mistrust and call it what it is. Then take an even harder look into His burning eyes of love and know that all He wants for you is total and complete freedom. He wants it more than you want it for yourself. So trust that what He shows you is always and only for your absolute good.

CHAPTER CONFIDENCE KEYS: KNOWING WHO YOU ARE IN GOD

1. God sees all the depths and layers of your heart—the good, the bad, and the ugly. And yet even in this He is unashamed to call you His own. If you are in Christ, He has wed himself to you fully knowing your weakness. He loves you and doesn't see you the way you see you. Let this be your confession: He loves you right now, today, in this moment, and will continue to do so forever and ever. And what He sees in you, He calls beautiful.

2. God has set you free both *from* things and *for* things. You are free *from* bondage so that you can be free *for* freedom. You are free *from* your past so that you may be free *for* a destiny He has designed just for you. He has set you free *from* the conformity of religious society so you can be free *for* unique expression to worship Him. Freedom is both a *from* and *for* victory. Be sure to learn about both sides!

Chapter 8

IN CLOSING: LEARNING
TO BE A LISTENER

The lessons I learned in the garden of prayer are lessons I carry with me at all times. No, I cannot automatically remember every detail, but the details are there just the same. No, I cannot always remember every word of every conversation, but the truths are there just the same. All of these lessons are treasures hidden in the field of my heart (Matthew 13:44). At just the moment it is needed, the Spirit helps me recall what He has taught me under our tree (John 14:26). He helps me excavate the treasure from the soil of my spirit (Matthew 13:52).

I believe God made me a visual learner and therefore uses vision to speak to me. He wants me to easily learn how to hear Him speak. He's not trying to hide and make knowing Him difficult. He wants me to hear Him! Because He made each of us different, I believe some people will be more apt to hear God in certain ways while others will hear Him in differing ways. Visual learners will probably be more apt to see vision and dreams. Audible learners will be more able to hear Him speaking internally or by hearing distinct sounds in the Spirit.

However, God is also a God of variety, so He likes to teach us in ways that aren't our most natural mode of learning. I believe He does this to stretch our faith, mature our relationship, and simply keep us dependent on Him and not on a "system" of hearing. We should, therefore, be open to unexpected ways of hearing God speak: whether through vision, circumstances, individuals, or whatever mode He chooses. Although I am a visual communicator, some of the most precious times I have with the Lord in journaling are when I hear more than I see. These moments are precious

WE SHOULD, THEREFORE, BE OPEN TO UNEXPECTED WAYS OF HEARING GOD SPEAK: WHETHER THROUGH VISION, CIRCUMSTANCES, INDIVIDUALS, OR WHATEVER MODE HE CHOOSES.

because the words just flow in an endless conversation. By faith, I just begin to write and the words follow one after another, words filled with wisdom and insight that I know comes from the Father. So whether He is speaking one day in vision and the next day through words, this much I know: He *is* speaking. My part is to open my heart to simply listen.

The eyes that will keep looking in prayer and the ears that will keep listening in prayer will find layers of truth in every story, every vision, and every word the Lord shares. This is true of every lesson I have learned by our tree. Just under the surface of the revelation He shares with me is a flowing stream, a stream that ties all of the revelations, all of the Scripture reading, all of the prayers together with another truth: the truth that God is good, that He is a loving Father who is always teaching the child who will but spend time with Him. The heart that will yield to Him will find a God who is tender, loving, and wise, as He is holy, righteous, and just. What I used to think of as different sides of God's personality I now understand as simply *God*. It is the same Spirit who is holy as the Spirit who is love as the Spirit who is fearsome as the Spirit who is compassionate! This is God—our God—true and righteous, Father and friend. He is not divided into segments or traits; He is *all in all* (Song of Songs 5:16; 1 Corinthians 12:6; Ephesians 1:23). The more we awaken to all of who He is, the more we awaken in wonder and worship.

My time with Him under our tree has only caused me to hunger to know Him—to *really* know Him—as He is. The more I gaze on Him and see how good He is, the more I long to know His severity (Romans 11:22). The more I gaze on Him and see how fearsome He is, the more I am filled with love for Him (Nehemiah 1:5). What appear to my human mind as contradictions are united in one all-powerful, all-holy, altogether lovely God. Like Nehemiah, I cry out, "Our God, you are powerful, fearsome, and faithful, always true to your word" (Nehemiah 9:32, CEV). May I never shy away from any "side" of God. May my heart ever be open to say, "Oh God, who is an all-consuming fire, fill me with the knowledge of you!"

The lessons under the tree have taught me that God is longing to find a friend. He is longing for an ear to listen to Him and longing to lend an ear to listen. This is the truth we learn in the garden called Eden. God was overflowing with such love He could not help but create a friend who was just like Him, someone with whom He could walk and talk in the cool of the day. I believe God taught the first man and woman in that garden about His nature, inviting them into the knowledge of Him by way of deepening friendship. He wasn't merely shooting the breeze with them on those walks together! He was breaking the bread of fellowship that their hearts might burn to know Him more. The

> FROM THAT GARDEN WE LEARN THAT GOD IS AN INTIMATE FRIEND WHO DOESN'T CAST US OFF EVEN IN OUR FAILURE, BUT ONE WHO MAKES A WAY FOR OUR SHAME TO BE COVERED AND OUR SINS FORGIVEN.

more that fire burned on their hearts, the less the enemy could cast a shadow of doubt on their hearts.

From that garden we learn that God is an intimate friend who doesn't cast us off even in our failure, but One who makes a way for our shame to be covered and our sins forgiven. This is the truth that echoed out of Eden to the mountain of Horeb. Although the walk in the cool of the day was replaced by a mountain burning with fire surrounded by a thundering storm, for the few who would swallow their fear and step into the flame, they found that at the heart of the fearsome display was the same God who had called them in Eden. The cry was the same in the garden as it was on the mountain: "Come to me to find real life."

Through all of the law and all of the prophets, this call continued, echoing through the songs of David, through the tears of Jeremiah, and through the proclamation of John the Baptist. When God's Son entered the world, the call from Eden echoed in every word He spoke, every miracle He performed, and every tear He cried. His very life echoed the call because He *was* the call. Jesus was the heart of the Father manifested on earth. God, in flesh, walking with man once again in the cool of the day—teaching us, drawing us into the knowledge of God.

To some, the call of God through the life of Jesus was like a lovely song sung by one with a pleasant voice: something to be listened to and enjoyed, but then easily forgotten (Ezekiel 33:32; Matthew 11:16-19). For others, the call was an offense, an unexpected cry that awakens them from their slumber only to arouse their wrath (Matthew 21:12-16; John 5:25-29). For the few who had ears to hear—I mean, *really* hear—they found a light that broke through the shadows of doubt. They were able to look past the Tree of the Knowledge of Good and Evil to the Tree of Life to learn the true knowledge of God. These are the ones who heard the call: "Come to me and I will give you rest" (Matthew 11:28).

Being willing to come to Him and receive from the Lord in new ways is a key to developing greater trust, greater maturity, and, I believe, greater authority in the spirit. The Lord speaks in so many varying ways. Let us always be listening with our ears as well as our eyes, our mind, our emotions, our conversations with others, and through whatever modes of communication God uses.

The Lord loves to communicate, so let's listen with all we are, knowing that every word He speaks is for our good. Let us keep open ears and open eyes and therefore be perpetual students who are ever learning from our Master the lessons He teaches.

Until the day we truly see Him face to face and are free from seeing "in part" and "through a glass dimly" (1 Corinthians 13:9-12), may we all gather with Jesus in ever-growing expectation under the shade of Grace.

ENDNOTES

1 Mark Virkler, *How to Hear God's Voice* (Shippensburg: Destiny Image Publishers, 2005).

2 Mike Bickle, *The Song of Songs* (Kansas City: Forerunner Books, 2007), p. 52.

3 David Ruis, *Live Worship: Touching the Father's Heart* (Mercy/Vineyard Publishing, 1994).

4 Ludwig van Beethoven (1770-1827), "Ode to Joy," from Symphony No. 9, 1824.